MOUNT WHITNEY

MOUNT WHITNEY

The Complete Trailhead-to-Summit Hiking Guide

Paul Richins, Jr.

Foreword by Steve Roper

THE
MOUNTAINEERS
BOOKS

Published by
The Mountaineers Books
1001 SW Klickitat Way, Suite 201
Seattle, WA 98134

Published simultaneously in Great Britain by Cordee, 3a DeMontfort Street, Leicester, England, LE1 7HD

Manufactured in the United States of America

Project Editor: Julie Van Pelt
Editor: Carol Anne Peschke
Cover and Book Designer: Kristy L. Welch
Layout Artist: Kristy L. Welch
Mapmaker: Ben Pease
Photographer: All photographs by Paul Richins, Jr., except where noted

Cover photograph: *East face of Mount Whitney as viewed from Upper Boy Scout Lake* © Galen Rowell/CORBIS
Title page: *Mount Whitney viewed from near Lone Pine along the Whitney Portal Road*
Frontispiece: *Mount Whitney and the Mountaineers Route, viewed from near the Russell–Carillon Pass*
Page 6: *Crooks Peak, Keeler Needle, and the east face of Mount Whitney from the North Fork Lone Pine Creek (Routes 4 and 5).* Page 17: *Approaching the east face of Mount Whitney below Upper Boy Scout Lake (Routes 4 and 5).* Page 35: *Mirror Lake on the Mount Whitney Trail (Route 6).* Page 51: *Hamilton Lake with Kaweah Gap in the background (Route 11).* Page 59: *Superb scenery on the High Sierra Trail looking toward Kaweah Gap (Route 11).* Page 75: *University Peak from Kearsarge Pass Trail (Route 1).* Page 143: *Bridge across the South Fork Kings River (Route 10).*

Library of Congress Cataloging-in-Publication Data
Richins, Paul, 1949-
  Mount Whitney : the complete trailhead-to-summit hiking guide / Paul Richins, Jr.—1st ed.
      p. cm.
  Includes bibliographical references (p.   ) and index.
  ISBN 0-89886-766-5
  1. Hiking—California—Whitney, Mount—Guidebooks. 2. Whitney, Mount (Calif.)—Guidebooks. I. Title: Mt. Whitney. II. Title.
  GV199.42.C22 W455 2001
  917.94'86—dc21

                                                                                    00-012473

Dedicated to my good friend Gene Leach,

who at ages 65, 68, and 71 hiked Routes 8, 3, and 4,

climbing Mounts Langley, Whitney, Tyndall, Williamson,

Russell, and Muir (peaks over 14,000 feet).

And at age 73,

less than four months after quadruple heart bypass surgery,

completed the Circumnavigation Route of Whitney (Route 4),

ascending Mount Russell and Mount Whitney en route.

More recently, at age 76,

he rode his mountain bike and hiked to the top of

White Mountain (third highest peak in California)

as a tune-up for Route 9, in which he carried

a full pack to Trail Crest (13,600 feet) before hiking

to the summit of Whitney.

Gene has been a true friend and inspiration to me.

▲   ▲   ▲

CONTENTS

Chapter 6: Westside Trailheads

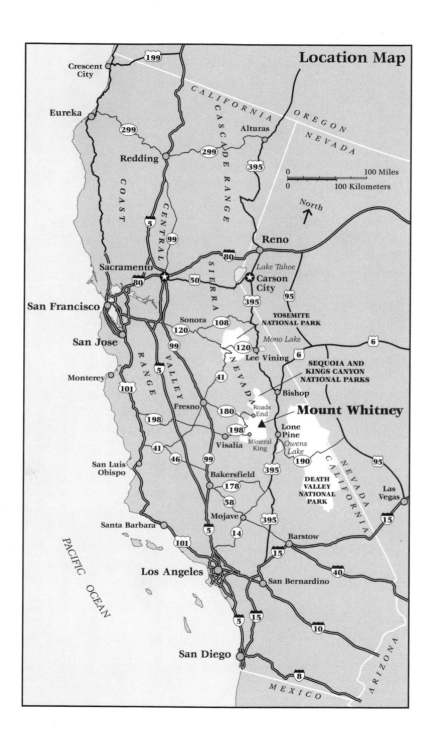

Key to Map and Graph Symbols

—●—	Featured trail with route number
···●···	Cross-country route with route number
--●--	Trail featured in other chapter
—~—·	John Muir Trail or Pacific Crest Trail
---~---	Other trail
═══5═══	Interstate highway
—(395)—	U.S. highway
—(198)—	State highway
———	Paved road
———	Dirt road
♠	Ranger station or patrol cabin
▬	Bear-proof food storage box
	Special areas
—·—·—	Boundary
○	Trailhead
▲	Campground
◎	Town
▪	Building
·	Point of interest
▴ ▲	Peaks
)(	Pass
—	Ridge
—	River or stream
—	Waterfall
◇	Lake
This Map / Other Maps	Key to adjoining maps

FOREWORD

In 1954 I approached the top of Mount Whitney as a pilgrim might approach Mecca. Having dreamed of this moment for several years, I raced up that final level path with my heart thumping—and not just from the altitude.

I had been lucky enough to attend the first-ever Sierra Club Wilderness Base Camp, and one of the lures of this 10-day outing was the possibility of climbing Whitney at the end, if the weather cooperated. It did, and that stifling August day still sparks my memory. How thrilled I was to stand on the highest spot in the Lower 48! Far below, to the east, the dull Owens Valley quivered in the haze. In the other three directions rose uncountable peaks, nameless and unclimbed as far as I knew. This wasn't true, but the mystery seized me. My mountaineering career began at this very moment. I was 13.

I've been back to those sere summit rocks three times since, by various routes. Much of the attraction, of course, is that the highest spot of the contiguous 48 states is a desirable goal simply because of its preeminent position. Yet Whitney's human history also draws me in. The striplings King and Cotter named the mountain for their boss but ended up on the wrong peak, and Josiah Whitney must have been both pleased and pained. King's later failures even now make us cringe. John Muir's shunning of the easy way up makes us aware of challenges then and now. The Smithsonian experiments cause us to ponder the heavens. The pioneering ascent of the formidable east face alerts us to the "impossible." All these stories, so well related by Paul Richins in this book, add spice to the ascent, no matter which route you take.

Although the summit of Whitney is the end result of each hike described herein, it's the chase rather than the conquest that will appeal to many readers. Days might go by before you reach the summit, and these might well be the best days of your life. The interior of the High Sierra, invisible from any road and visited by few people, is one of the magical spots on our planet. Elegant lakes occupy grand cirques. Streams of diamond clarity dart toward the canyons below. Marmots whistle from the talus, and mountain bluebirds hawk for insects near their nests in golden snags. Wildflowers. Meadows. Paradise.

Many of the routes Richins has chosen lie in timber line country, the narrow zone lying between the lowland forests and the naked crags above. Traveling through this region usually is easy, and the vistas are endless. On a clear day—which is the rule during the summer and early fall—you can reach out and touch peaks a dozen miles away, or so it seems. Sometimes thunderstorms disturb the calm, and shadows race each other across the landscape. The mountains tremble and the wind howls. What a time to be setting up camp and gazing out into a true wilderness!

Paul Richins knows this region as few do. His love for the Range of Light shines on every page, and I hope that more books from him are in the offing. I'll look forward to them.

Steve Roper

PREFACE

Ascending Mount Whitney by one of the thirteen hiking routes described in this guidebook is not technically difficult but requires good planning, stamina, and persistence. Whether you have climbed the peak before or are planning your first ascent, this guidebook will equip you with the necessary information for a safe and enjoyable trip.

In a typical year, about 30,000 hikers secure a wilderness permit to climb Mount Whitney. Many others are less fortunate and fail to obtain a permit for various reasons. Of these 30,000 hikers, only one in three reach the summit, a high attrition rate considering the excellent trails to the top. This guidebook will increase your chances of securing a wilderness permit and improve the likelihood of a successful trip.

What distinguishes *Mount Whitney: The Complete Trailhead-to-Summit Hiking Guide* from the other hiking guidebooks is that it not only includes the popular Mount Whitney Trail (Route 6) but also features twelve other trails and cross-country hiking routes. These routes traverse some of the most magnificent terrain imaginable and are far removed from the hundreds of hikers swarming the Mount Whitney Trail. Besides the wilderness experience of using a route other than the Mount Whitney Trail, an added benefit is that the odds of securing a wilderness permit are greatly increased. Selecting any of the hiking routes described in this guide will result in an outstanding trip. However, the Circumnavigation Route of Mount Whitney (Route 4), New Army Pass Route (Route 8), and High Sierra Trail (Route 11) are my favorites because they attract fewer hikers and pass through some of the most outstanding alpine terrain in California.

With the late Walt Wheelock's *Climbing Mount Whitney* guidebook in hand, I first hiked the Mount Whitney Trail over the Thanksgiving holiday break from school. That was more than 30 years ago, and, needless to say, I was the only one on the mountain that icy, cold November day. The temperature dropped to 12 degrees Fahrenheit at my tent at Trail Camp. That morning, as I labored up the ninety-seven snow-covered switchbacks to Trail Crest, I was impressed with and inspired by the mountain's solitude and rugged beauty.

Years later I returned with my daughter, Sierra. At age 10 she hiked Route 8, climbing Cirque Peak by moonlight, Mount Langley, and Mount Whitney, on consecutive days. Just as I was inspired years earlier by Mount Whitney's magnificence, Sierra was equally motivated. As we descended the ninety-seven switchbacks, she vowed to climb all the 14,000-footers in California. This she accomplished by age 13.

With a trail to the top, no one is too young or too old to make an attempt. In so doing, you too may be inspired to new personal heights.

I hope you enjoy the guidebook and have many opportunities to climb this magnificent mountain by several different routes. Your feedback is encouraged. Please send your comments to my email address, *prichins@jps.net,* or view my website, Backcountry Resource Center, at *http://pweb.jps.net/~prichins/backcountry_resource_center.htm.* Happy hiking!

Paul Richins, Jr.

A NOTE ABOUT SAFETY

There are inherent risks in hiking, climbing, and backpacking: Rockfall, snowstorms, snow slides, rain, high winds, thunderstorms, lightning, hypothermia, mountain sickness, bears, and the unexpected all pose varying hazards for the backcountry traveler. Although the author and publisher have done their best to provide accurate information, conditions change from day to day and from year to year. It is presumed that the users of this guidebook possess the requisite hiking, climbing, and backpacking skills for safe travel in the mountains and are proficient in using compass and map for navigation. The author and publisher disclaim any liability for injury or other damage by anyone hiking, backpacking, climbing, or camping in areas described in this guidebook or traveling to and from these outings.

Safety is an important concern in all outdoor activities. No guidebook can alert you to every hazard or anticipate the limitations of every reader. Therefore, the descriptions of roads, trails, routes, and natural features in this book are not representations that a particular place or excursion is safe for your party. When you follow any of the routes described in this book, you assume responsibility for your own safety. Under normal conditions, such excursions demand the usual attention to traffic, road and trail conditions, weather, terrain, the capabilities of your party, and other factors. Keeping informed about current conditions and exercising common sense are the keys to a safe, enjoyable outing.

The Mountaineers Books

AUTHOR'S NOTE

Mount Whitney: The Complete Trailhead-to-Summit Hiking Guide features thirteen hiking routes culminating in the summit of Whitney. Eight of the thirteen routes follow well-maintained trails over their entire length. The five others involve limited cross-country travel in combination with hiking over established trails. Route titles containing the word *Trail*, as in *Kearsarge Pass Trail*, involve trail hiking only. Those with the word *Route*, as in *University Pass Route*, involve some cross-country travel along with trail hiking. In this guidebook, the words *climb* and *climbing* are used throughout in the context of hiking and backpacking. No technical rock climbing skills involving rope management and mountain hardware are necessary for the trails and hiking routes described herein.

The cross-country routes described in this guidebook (Routes 2, 4, 5, 7, and 8) are considerably more difficult than the hikes that follow trails over their entire length (Routes 1, 3, 6, and 9-13). The cross-country routes should not be attempted by hikers with little or no previous routefinding experience. Inexperienced hikers lacking proficiency in the use of a compass and map may easily find themselves off route and on dangerously steep terrain. The Mountaineers Route (Route 5) and Meysan Lake Route (Route 7) are particularly difficiult and should only be attempted by experienced backcountry hikers.

ACKNOWLEDGMENTS

Hiking the featured trails, photographing the splendid scenery, and finally writing *Mount Whitney: The Complete Trailhead-to-Summit Hiking Guide* has been a delight. An additional, much appreciated pleasure was the assistance I received from Colin Fuller, Jan Cutts, Diana Pietrasanta, Peter Stevens, Ward Eldridge, and Steve Roper. A special thanks is extended to each of them.

Colin Fuller, M.D., provided valuable assistance in writing the Chapter 2 sections on hypothermia, mountain sickness, dehydration, water purification, sunburn, and snow blindness and Appendix 3, Contents of a Wilderness First-Aid Kit. His experience and knowledge of the subject matter are extensive.

Jan Cutts and Diana Pietrasanta, with the Inyo National Forest, supplied extensive information on the U.S. Forest Service wilderness permit process and provided data and statistics on trail usage. Their assistance was especially important because the Forest Service implemented an entirely new permit and quota system while this guidebook was being written. Their review of Chapter 4 sections on wilderness permits and regulations is greatly appreciated.

Peter Stevens and Ward Eldridge, staff with Sequoia National Park, provided information on wilderness permit procedures and a list and locations of wilderness bear-proof food storage boxes. Ward Eldridge also reviewed archived Mount Whitney summit registers for the number of climbers recording their accomplishment. Their assistance in providing this critical data was highly beneficial.

Heartfelt thanks are extended to Steve Roper for the exquisite Foreword. Steve Roper is a well-known author of mountaineering books, including *Camp 4: Recollections of a Yosemite Rockclimber*, *The High Sierra Route: Traversing Timberline Country*, and *Fifty Classic Climbs of North America*. His insight and encouragement, on this and other projects, are greatly valued.

▲ Chapter 1 ▲

Introduction to the Sierra Nevada and Mount Whitney

From the small town of Lone Pine, the precipitously rugged east face escarpment of the Sierra Nevada rises more than 10,000 feet from the desert floor to the popular summit of Mount Whitney, the highest peak in the Lower 48. The short drive from Lone Pine to Whitney Portal reveals dramatic views of Whitney's east face and glimpses of the splendor of the Sierra Nevada wilderness. However, to fully appreciate all that the mountain has to offer, experience the wilderness first hand: hike backcountry trails, explore lush meadows and streams, camp alongside alpine lakes, and scramble up Whitney's inviting slopes. You will come away from the experience refreshed and invigorated.

California's Sierra Nevada is a unique and unforgettable land of high adventure and enjoyment, a hiker's haven stretching nearly the length of the state. From Lake Tahoe and the Desolation Valley Wilderness Area in the north to Mount Whitney and the John Muir Wilderness Area in the south, this unbroken chain of mountains offers an endless variety of outdoor opportunities. Picturesque alpine lakes, scenic meadows, colorful wildflowers, cascading streams, deep river canyons, elegant arêtes, sheer granite faces, precipitous couloirs, immense glacial cirques, lofty mountain passes, and splendid summits inspire the backcountry wilderness traveler.

Much has been written about the inspiring California landscapes and the Sierra Nevada, but Clarence King said it best when he wrote,

By far the grandest of all the ranges is the Sierra Nevada, a long and massive uplift lying between the arid deserts of the Great Basin and the Californian exuberance of grainfield and orchard; its eastern slope, a defiant wall of rock plunging abruptly down to the plain; the western, a long, grand sweep, well watered and overgrown with cool, stately forests; its crest a line of sharp, snowy peaks springing into the sky and catching the alpenglow long after the sun has set for all the rest of America.

Clarence King, *Mountaineering in the Sierra Nevada*, 1872

The Sierra Nevada begins near Lassen Volcanic National Park and continues south to Mount Whitney ending at Tehachapi Pass. The range runs generally north and south along the eastern side of the state, forming California's geographic backbone. The Sierra Nevada gradually increases in elevation from north to south in a surprisingly orderly manner. The highest peaks in the north, near Lake Tahoe, barely reach 10,000 feet. Moving south along the crest of the range, higher and higher peaks are encountered: 11,000-foot peaks appear for the first time near Sonora Pass (Highway 108), 12,000-footers begin east of Bridgeport in the Sawtooth area, and 13,000-foot summits initially emerge in the Yosemite high country. The first 14,000-foot peak is not encountered until the Palisades region, 250 miles south of the start of the range. Five of the Sierra Nevada's eleven 14,000-foot peaks are located in the Palisades region. These magnificent peaks are soon followed by the remaining six 14,000-foot peaks of the Whitney region. The Sierra Nevada culminates atop Mount Whitney. Six miles to the south is Mount Langley, the last 14,000-foot peak in

The east face escarpment of the Sierra Nevada, with Mount Whitney in the background

the Sierra Nevada. From this point, the peaks rapidly decrease in elevation, and the Sierra Nevada ends near Mojave.

Within a 6-mile radius of Whitney, five other majestic peaks (Mounts Tyndall, Williamson, Russell, Muir, and Langley) tower above the magical 14,000-foot level (see Appendix 1 for a list of California's fourteeners). From the summits of these beautiful peaks, the grandeur of the Sierra Nevada stretches as far as the eye can see, miles and miles of rock on rock, mountain on mountain.

The beauty and size of the mountain range are unparalleled. The Sierra Nevada's splendor is exemplified by Lake Tahoe and three fabulous national parks: Yosemite National Park, Sequoia National Park, and Kings Canyon National Park. The range's size and scale are enormous. To provide a sense of geographic perspective, the Sierra Nevada easily exceeds the size of the entire European Alps: the French, Swiss, Austrian, and Italian Alps combined.

The height of Mount Whitney has been the subject of much speculation and debate over the years. Using the best barometer technology of the 1870s, John Muir noted in his writings that the elevation of Whitney approached 14,700 feet. More recent measurements and publications have reported the elevation to be 14,501 feet, 14,497 feet, 14,496 feet, and 14,494 feet. The summit sign placed on September 5, 1930, commemorating the completion of the John Muir Trail, "the highest trail in the United States," fixed the elevation at 14,496.811 feet. However, the most recent U.S. Geological Survey (USGS) 7.5-minute map establishes the height of the summit at 4416.9 meters (3.2808 feet per meter x 4416.9 meters = 14,490.97 feet).

At 14,491 feet, Mount Whitney is the highest peak in the Sierra Nevada as well as the 48 contiguous states. Hikers from throughout California, the United States, and the world covet the privilege of standing on its prestigious summit. All this attention makes Whitney the most frequently climbed peak in the Sierra Nevada as 30,000 hikers attempt the peak each year by various trails (see Appendix 6).

Each summer and fall, a wide assortment of hikers attempt the peak. I have observed an unsteady 80-year-old woman with tattered tennis shoes and no socks inching her way up the trail without even a walking stick for assistance; joggers wearing shorts and windbreakers with water bottles in hand; backpackers with all types of unnecessary gear strapped to the outside of their overburdened packs; discouraged hikers at 14,000 feet, blue around the gills, looking and feeling as if they were going to die from the effects of the altitude; and fathers with young children starting out at Whitney Portal with high hopes of summiting. And, of course, many well-qualified and experienced hikers complete the hike with little difficulty.

HISTORY

The Sierra Nevada was formed over many millions of years through a series of uplifts that pushed the great Sierra Block upward and tilted it toward the west. From a geologic perspective, the range is essentially a gigantic granite block 350 miles long and 40 to 80 miles wide that has been tilted on its side. While the Sierra Block was being pushed upward, the land to the east began to drop thousands of feet, creating the impressive east face of the range that is readily seen from US 395. This explains why the east side of this range is so rugged and sheer, whereas the slopes on the west gradually rise to the summit over many miles.

Mount Shasta was known as early as 1788, Mount Rainier and Mount Hood were identified in 1792, but Whitney was not discovered until July 2, 1864. Mount Whitney was first sighted by William Brewer and Charles Hoffman of the Whitney Survey Field Party from Mount Brewer, nearly 15 miles to the north. Mount Whitney cannot be seen from the San Joaquin Valley to the west and can be observed from only a limited number of points from the east. When viewed from the east near Lone Pine, the mountain does not dominate the view, nor is it readily apparent that it is the highest peak in the range. John Muir compared the relative obscurity of Mount Whitney with the dominance of Mount Shasta in an article titled "Snow-Storm on Mount Shasta," appearing in *Harper's New Monthly Magazine,* September 1877. He had spent the night of April 30, 1875, on the summit of Mount Shasta in a perilous blizzard with little more than a shirt when he wrote,

Go where you will within a radius of from fifty to a hundred miles, there stands the colossal cone of Shasta, clad in perpetual snow, the one grand landmark that never sets. While Mount Whitney, situated near the southern extremity of the Sierra, notwithstanding it lifts its granite summit some four or five hundred feet higher than Shasta, is yet almost entirely snowless during the summer months, and is so feebly individualized, the traveller often searches for it in vain amid the thickets of rival peaks by which it is surrounded.

Nevertheless, Clarence King's passion to be the first to climb the highest peak in the land resulted in three failed attempts in the 1860s and early 1870s. His two most notable attempts were in 1864 and 1871. In July 1864, after spotting Mount Whitney from high on the shoulder of Mount Brewer, he set out for the peak, 15 miles to the south. After several days of cross-country travel over rugged terrain, he mistakenly climbed Mount Tyndall (6 miles north of his goal). In 1871 he made a similar mistake by climbing Mount Langley (6 miles south of his goal) and proclaiming that he had climbed the highest peak in the land. It was an overcast day and he could not see Whitney a short distance away. We may cringe at King's navigational skills and his sensational storytelling, but his accomplishments, given the knowledge of the terrain at the time, were impressive.

Two years later, on August 18, 1873, Whitney was finally climbed by three local fishermen from Lone Pine: Charley Begole, Johnny Lucas, and Al Johnson. They named the peak Fisherman's Peak, but the name did not stick. Clarence King at last climbed the peak on September 19, 1873. When he reached the summit he was disappointed to learn that he was not the first but rather the tenth one up (see Appendix 6).

On October 21 of that same year, John Muir made the first ascent of what is today called the Mountaineers Route (Route 5). Hope Broughton, Mary Martin, Anna Mills, and Mrs. Redd (her first name was not recorded) were the first women to reach the summit, climbing the peak in 1878. They approached the peak from the west, coming all the way from Visalia on horseback. At the base of the mountain, possibly near Crabtree Meadow or Guitar Lake, they left their horses and ascended the peak's west slopes. The other major peaks in the region were soon climbed, with the exception of Mount Russell, which because of its difficult rock faces and exposed ridges was not climbed until 1926 by Norman Clyde.

In 1904, the people of Lone Pine raised the necessary funds to build a horse trail to the summit, which they rebuilt and repaired in 1909. This trail allowed the Smithsonian Institution to erect a stone shelter near the top for use by their astronomers and other scientists. Mount Whitney became the site of many scientific experiments in the late 1800s and early 1900s. The U.S. Weather Service conducted experiments and observations on the summit for 20 years. The hut is still used today as an emergency shelter but was the site of at least

Hamilton Lake looking toward Kaweah Gap on the High Sierra Trail (Route 11)

one lightning strike death of a hiker who took refuge there during a thunderstorm. The shelter has since been grounded but is not considered safe during a thunder and lightning storm.

The Mount Whitney Trail was again rebuilt and realigned in 1928–30. After World War II, the Forest Service realigned the trail one last time. With the aid of a large compressor, an excellent trail with its ninety-seven switchbacks was blasted from the rocky buttress between Trail Camp and Trail Crest. This new route, the route used today, bypassed the snowfields that had often blocked the old trail until late summer.

During the time the Mount Whitney Trail was being built and rebuilt the residents of the area formed the "Inyo Better Roads Club." It was the group's goal to improve US 395, as the journey from Los Angeles took 2 days. As the roads improved in the early years of the century, the Eastern Sierra became a Hollywood playground. Actor Lon Chaney built a cabin on Pine Creek under the Palisades, and Rock Creek Lodge became known as "Little Switzerland." Many Western movies were filmed east of Lone Pine just off the Whitney Portal Road on Movie Road A and B, and automobile and truck commercials are still filmed in the area.

The popularity of the peak has grown over the past 40 years, as evidenced by those recording their names in the summit register. In 1957, 2658 signed the summit register. By 2000 this number had increased to approximately 10,200 (see Appendix 6).

HOW TO USE THIS GUIDEBOOK

Whether you have climbed the peak before or are planning your first attempt, *Mount Whitney: The Complete Trailhead-to-Summit Hiking Guide* will equip you with the necessary information for a safe, enjoyable, and successful trip. The critical information of what to expect, what to take, when to go, planning tips, and wilderness permit requirements is explained in Chapters 1 through 4. In Chapter 5 (Eastside Trailheads) and Chapter 6 (Westside Trailheads) thirteen terrific hiking routes for your trip to the top are thoroughly described. Of the thirteen routes, nine begin on the east side of the Sierra Nevada crest and four begin on the west side of the crest in Sequoia and Kings Canyon National Parks.

The following chart summarizes the thirteen hiking routes described in this guidebook.

Trail Name	Rating	Mileage (to the summit)	Elevation Gain	Effort Factor	Duration
Eastside Trailheads					
1. Kearsarge Pass Trail	Class 1	39.2 miles	10,771 feet	30.4 hours	5–7 days
2. University Pass Route	Class 2	32.1 miles	10,711 feet	26.8 hours	5–7 days
3. Shepherd Pass Trail	Class 1	29.0 miles	10,951 feet	25.5 hours	4–6 days
4. Circumnavigation of Mount Whitney	Class 2	12.0 miles	7,686 feet	13.7 hours	4–6 days
5. Mountaineers Route	Class 3	4.7 miles	6,126 feet	8.5 hours	1–3 days
6. Mount Whitney Trail	Class 1	11.0 miles	6,306 feet	11.8 hours	1–3 days
7. Meysan Lake Route	Class 2	12.1 miles	8,971 feet	15.1 hours	4–6 days
8. New Army Pass Route	Class 2	18.1 miles	6,751 feet	15.9 hours	4–6 days
9. Cottonwood Pass Trail	Class 1	29.7 miles	7,341 feet	22.2 hours	4–6 days
Westside Trailheads					
10. Bubbs Creek Trail	Class 1	43.2 miles	12,776 feet	34.4 hours	5–7 days
11. High Sierra Trail	Class 1	61.1 miles	14,851 feet	45.5 hours	6–8 days
12. Franklin Pass Trail	Class 1	49.0 miles	12,371 feet	36.9 hours	5–7 days
13. Farewell Gap Trail	Class 1	59.3 miles	14,848 feet	44.6 hours	6–8 days

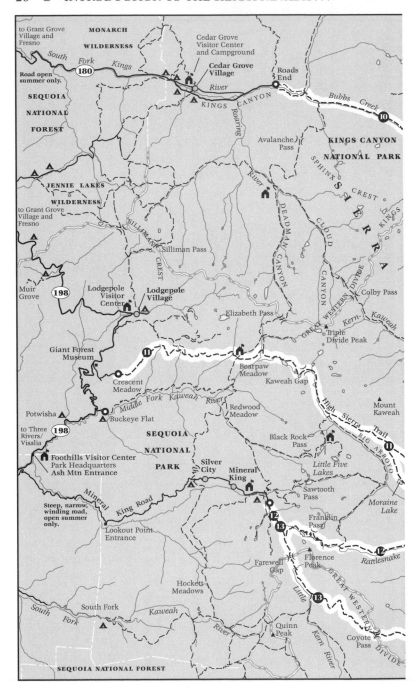

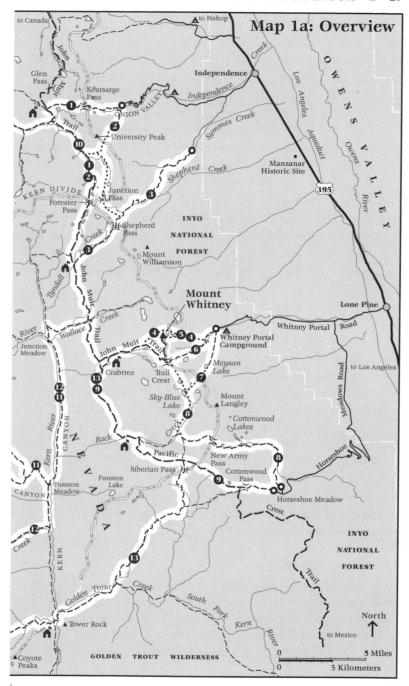

Map 1a: Overview

Of the thirteen trails/hiking routes, eight (Routes 1, 3, 6, and 9–13) follow well-maintained trails over their entire length to the summit. These hiking trails have a difficulty rating of Class 1. The remaining five (Routes 2, 4, 5, 7, and 8) entail limited cross-country travel in combination with trail hiking to reach the top and are rated Class 2 or Class 3 (see "The Ratings Explained" later in this chapter).

Generally, the approaches originating on the east side of the Sierra Nevada are shorter and start higher than the routes originating on the west side. Because of the topography of the Sierra Nevada, the east side is steep, with short approaches in a dry, desertlike climate created by the rain shadow of the Sierra Nevada. This is in stark contrast to the west side of the range, where the terrain is relatively gentle, the approaches are long, and the heavily timbered mountains receive copious amounts of rain and snow each year.

Access to the eastside trailheads is gained by east–west arterioles from Independence (Routes 1–3) or Lone Pine (Routes 4–9) on US 395. The four trailheads beginning on the west side of the Sierra Nevada crest start from Roads End in Kings Canyon National Park (Route 10), Crescent Meadow in Sequoia National Park (Route 11), and Mineral King in Sequoia National Park (Routes 12 and 13). Within each chapter the trails are presented from north to south.

Each hiking route description begins with a difficulty rating, the distance to the summit, the total elevation gain, an estimate of the amount of effort (in hours) necessary to reach the summit, the trip duration in days, suggested maps, and a trail profile table and graph. Each route is described with an "In a Nutshell" summary followed by a listing of the trailhead facilities, a description of how to get there, bear-proof food storage box locations, and a detailed narrative description of the trail and what you can expect along the way. Maps of each hiking route are also included.

The Ratings Explained

Each hiking route has been given a rating to describe its overall level of difficulty. The standard system for rating the difficulty of mountain climbs is called the Yosemite Decimal System. It was first introduced by the Sierra Club in 1937 and is still in use today. The system is a general guide to assist in determining the difficulty of a climb. It is geared to technical rock climbing, but the lower end of the scale is used to describe trail hiking, cross-country travel, and rock scrambling over uneven, difficult terrain. The rating system is as follows:

Class 1: Trail walking. This includes all the maintained trails covered in this guidebook: Routes 1, 3, 6, and 9–13.

Class 2: Includes hiking over uneven terrain, through brush, and up and around rock bluffs, steep gullies, scree (loose and sandy rock), and talus, where the hands may be needed for balance. This includes Routes 2, 4, 7, and 8.

Class 3: Terrain becomes steeper and the exposure increases. Arms and hands are used for balance and leverage. Handholds are easily identified. There is an increased risk of falling and being injured. Some inexperienced hikers may desire a roped belay over certain Class 3 terrain. Route 5 is the only route in the guidebook with Class 3 climbing. The route is predominantly Class 2, but there is a short Class 3 climbing section near the top.

Class 4: Terrain is steep and exposed. Most climbers need a rope for protection. Skill and a thorough knowledge of climbing procedure and rope techniques are necessary. Handholds are smaller and less defined. There is a greater risk of falling and injury. Falling could result in a broken leg or arm or even more serious injury. No Class 4 routes are described in the guide.

Class 5: This begins the ratings for the technical rock climbing using rope, helmet, and hardware. It demands experience and knowledge of climbing techniques and rope management. A fall could result in death. Class 5 climbing is broken into a decimal system of rating from 5.0 through 5.14. When climbing aid is necessary, an additional rating of A1 through A5 is used. The east face of Mount Whitney contains a number of classic 5.4 through 5.8 climbing routes. No Class 5 routes are described in this guidebook.

Distance to the Summit

The mileage detailed in this guide is approximate. To ensure accuracy, many sources were checked. Tom Harrison Maps, USGS 7.5-minute and 15-minute maps, U.S. Forest Service data, previously printed guidebooks, and trail mileage signs were consulted, with many discrepancies observed. No two sources seemed to agree on many of the basics of elevation and distance. The distance to the summit is an

The east face of Mount Whitney from near the Russell–Carillon Pass (Routes 4 and 5) Photo by Gene Leach

estimate of the mileage from the trailhead to the summit and does not include mileage for the return trip.

Elevation Gain

The elevations detailed in this guidebook are approximate. The elevation gain is the estimate of elevation increase from trailhead to the summit and does not include any elevation gained on the hike out.

Elevations are reported in feet. When a map or information source measures elevation in meters, meters have been converted to feet. The conversion factor used is meters times 3.2808 (39.37 inches/12 inches = 3.2808). For example, the USGS 7.5-minute map indicates that Mount Whitney is 4416.9 meters. To convert meters to feet, multiply 4416.9 meters by 3.2808 for a height of 14,490.97 feet, rounded to 14,491 feet.

Effort Factor

The effort factor formula gives the hiker a method to determine the amount of time (effort) necessary to hike from one point to another on a trail or cross-country route. Given the distance to be traveled (in miles) and the elevation to be gained (in feet), the overall effort (time in hours) needed to reach the summit can be estimated.

The formula is a refinement of Naismith's formula. In 1892, Scottish climber W. W. Naismith developed a way to estimate route times in the Scottish Highlands and English Lake District by taking into account the distance to be walked and the elevation to be climbed.

The Naismith formula allows 1 hour for every 3 miles traveled plus 1 hour for every 2000 feet of elevation gained. With a heavy pack at the much higher elevations encountered in the Sierra Nevada, the Naismith formula is not particularly useful.

The effort factor used in this guidebook corrects for some of these differences and is as follows: time in hours = (distance hiked in miles/2 miles per hour) + (elevation gained in feet/1000 feet per hour).

It is assumed that a hiker in good shape, carrying a 35- to 40-pound pack (a pack weighing about 20 to 25 percent of one's body weight), can average about 2 miles per hour on level terrain and ascend at a rate of 1000 feet per hour. For example, the summit of Mount Whitney following the Mount Whitney Trail is 11 miles and a climb of 6306 feet. Applying the formula to this example, the effort factor is (11 miles/2 miles per hour) + (6306 feet/1000 feet per hour) = 5.5 hours + 6.3 hours = 11.8 hours. In this example, it will take about 11–12 hours to reach the summit. Of course, many other factors not reflected in this equation affect one's rate of travel in the mountains: the elevation of the peak, the weight of one's pack, the condition of the trails, the ruggedness of the cross-country terrain, the amount of brush along the route, and the hiker's condition and strength.

If you are climbing to the peak in a single day, a much lighter day pack will allow a faster pace. In this example, you may want to adjust the formula by estimating 2.5 miles an hour or even 3 miles per hour instead of 2 miles per hour. Assuming 3 miles per hour, the formula is 11 miles/3 mph + 6336 feet/1000 feet per hour, or 3.7 hours + 6.3 hours = 10 hours.

On shorter trips, a hiker in good condition may easily beat the time predicted by the formula. On long and more difficult trips over rugged terrain, the same hiker may take longer than predicted to reach the summit because the rate of progress slows over the course of an exhausting day. You can adjust this rule easily to suit your pace by assuming a slower or faster hiking rate and adjusting the rate of elevation gain. To adjust for a strong and fast hiker, one might assume 2.5 miles per hour and 1200 feet of elevation gain per hour. To adjust for a slower traveler, one might assume 2 miles per hour but reduce the rate of ascent to 750 feet per hour.

For the descent, ignore the elevation gain portion of the formula and simply figure 2–3 miles per hour.

Trip Duration

This is an estimate of the number of days it will take to complete each trip from start to finish. The distance, elevation gain, and effort factor have been calculated to the summit of Whitney, but not for the hike out. However, the estimate of trip duration (in days) also includes the time required to hike out via the Mount Whitney Trail with an overnight stay at either Trail Camp or Outpost Camp before finishing at Whitney Portal.

Maps

The maps in this book are for general reference. They highlight the various trails and hiking routes featured in the guidebook and include many geographic features such as prominent lakes, streams, meadows, ridges, and peaks. On the maps, established trails are distinguished from cross-country travel: dashed lines represent existing trails and dotted lines represent cross-country portions of a route.

Each route description lists the U.S. Geological Survey (USGS) maps that are needed for the trip, both the 1:24,000 scale (7.5-minute series) and the 1:62,500 scale (15-minute series). Unfortunately, the USGS no longer produces the 1:62,500 scale maps, where an inch equals a mile. The detail and scale of these maps are ideal for hikers and backpackers. The new USGS 7.5-minute maps, where 2⅝ inch equals a mile, provide more information than is necessary, and you may need to pack six or more maps at a time to adequately cover a multiday trip. There are several excellent sources of 1:62,500 scale topographic maps. Tom Harrison Maps and Wilderness Press produce fine maps at the desired scale. Wildflower Productions produces TOPO! Interactive Maps on CD-ROM. These maps can be purchased at Inyo National Forest Service offices, Sequoia and Kings Canyon National Parks offices, Sequoia Natural History Association, and backpacking stores (see Appendix 5 for more information).

Trail Profile Table

For descriptive purposes, each trail and cross-country hiking route has been broken into short segments. These convenient trail profile tables include the milepost (miles from the start), the elevation of the milepost, the amount of elevation change for the trail segment, the number of miles from the preceding milepost, and the grade of the trail measured in feet (gain or loss) per mile. To gauge the relative grade or slope of a trail segment, the following general guidelines are offered:

0–200 feet per mile: flat or nearly flat walking

201–500 feet per mile: gentle hiking

501–800 feet per mile: moderately steep

801–1200 feet per mile: steep

1201 + feet per mile: very steep

When a trail segment both gains *and* loses elevation, the trail grade is given as "up/down."

Trail Profile Graph

These graphs illustrate the ups and downs of the route and are handy references for what lies ahead on the trail. As with the maps, the graphs use dashed lines to represent existing trails and dotted lines to indicate those portions of the route that require cross-country travel.

In a Nutshell

This section contains an informative overview of the hike, describing the highlights in a few short paragraphs.

Trailhead Facilities

The type of facilities at or near the trailhead such as campgrounds, picnic areas, fishing ponds, stores, telephones, food, and other services are discussed.

Upper Boy Scout Lake from Mount Russell. Good campsites are located at the lower end of the lake (Routes 4 and 5). Photo by Gene Leach

How to Get There

This section provides driving directions to reach the trailhead and the condition of the roads. All roads to the trailheads are paved except for the Shepherd Pass Trail (Route 3). The dirt road to the Shepherd Pass trailhead is passable in a sedan (i.e., a high-clearance vehicle is not needed).

Bear-Proof Food Storage Box Locations

Each trail description lists and fully describes the locations of the various bear-proof food storage boxes that have been placed by the personnel of the Sequoia and Kings Canyon National Parks. Nearly forty bear-proof boxes have been placed along the routes described in this guide.

Narrative Description

Each trail and cross-country hiking route has been broken into short segments, and each segment is thoroughly described. The narrative description corresponds with the trail profile table and trail profile graph.

Five Bonus Peaks

Besides providing thorough descriptions of thirteen hiking routes to Whitney's summit, this guidebook provides complete descriptions for climbing the five other 14,000-footers in the region. Each bonus peak is accessible from at least one of the featured thirteen trails, affording an excellent opportunity to climb one or more of these 14,000-footers. Mount Tyndall (14,019 feet) and Mount Williamson (14,370 feet) can be ascended from Routes 1, 2, 3, and 10; Mount Russell (14,088 feet) can be attained from Routes 4 and 5; Mount Muir (14,012 feet) can be reached from all routes except Route 5; and Mount Langley (14,022 feet) is climbed from Route 8. In addition, the summits of four 14,000-foot subpeaks of Mount Whitney (Aiguille Extra, 14,042 feet; Third Needle, 14,107 feet; Crooks Peak—also known as Day Needle—14,173 feet; and Keeler Needle, 14,239 feet) can be attained by an easy scramble above the John Muir Trail. For a more comprehensive discussion of various routes on these bonus peaks, refer to *The Climber's Guide to the High Sierra,* by Steve Roper, and *The High Sierra: Peaks, Passes and Trails,* by R. J. Secor.

▲ Chapter 2 ▲

What to Expect

Mountaineering is one of the finest sports imaginable but to practise it without technique is a form of more or less deliberate suicide. Technique encourages prudence; it also obviates fatigue and useless or dangerous halts and, far from excluding it, it permits meditation. It is not an end in itself but the means of promoting safety as much in the individual climb as on the rope.
Gaston Rébuffat, from *On Snow and Rock*

By knowing in advance what to expect, the dangers of mountain travel can be avoided and the problems mastered. Adverse weather, hypothermia, mountain sickness, dehydration, unsafe water, sunburn, snow blindness, lightning, bears, and other critters may be encountered. These and other wilderness issues are fully discussed below, including advice on how to cope with each potential problem.

TRAIL CONDITIONS

You can expect to find well-maintained, heavily used trails with a lot of hikers heading for the summit. The Forest Service and National Park

Service trails in the region provide various routes that almost any person in good shape can successfully ascend. However, if you are expecting an undemanding hike, stay home because the trek is strenuous by any trail. Though not technically difficult, all trails are challenging, demanding a good measure of stamina and persistence. Obviously some trails are less arduous than others. The less strenuous trails are Routes 1, 6, 9, and 10.

In addition to those routes following well-maintained trails, the guidebook features five hiking routes that involve limited amounts of cross-country travel. On these routes you can expect to see spectacular scenery, some of the best in the Sierra Nevada, and significantly fewer people. A hiker with a basic understanding of routefinding with a map and compass should be able to negotiate these cross-country routes. They follow creeks and traverse mountain passes that are clearly identifiable. With the proper use of global positioning systems (GPSs), cross-country travel and routefinding are greatly simplified. The GPS is a handy navigational tool if used correctly.

Early in the hiking season (June), the upper trail segments may be loaded with snow. In a heavy snow year it may be well into July before the trails are free of snow. Crampons and an ice ax may be necessary. For example, the ninety-seven switchbacks above Trail Camp on the Mount Whitney Trail (Route 6) and the south side of Forester Pass (Routes 1, 2, and 10) may become a bit tricky when the steep slopes are covered with snow. An early season ascent by way of Route 9 may be the best way to avoid the steep snow. Check with the National Park Service for trail conditions. If you plan to descend the Mount Whitney Trail, check on its condition as well.

WEATHER

The weather during the primary hiking season, June through October, usually is mild, clear, and sunny. However, the weather in the Sierra Nevada changes rapidly. When ascending a 14,000-foot peak, prepare for rapid changes in the temperature and weather, both from trailhead to summit and from one day to the next.

Additionally, over a 24-hour period there are wide temperature fluctuations. Evenings normally are pleasant and mild. However, during the night and early morning it is not unusual for the temperature to drop below freezing at camps above 11,000 feet. One may need to be warmly dressed when setting out for the summit in the early morning, but it may become short-sleeve weather by late morning or early afternoon. Conversely, a warm and sunny day can quickly change by late afternoon with the formation of huge thunderheads.

There is also great variability in weather and temperature from trailhead to summit. A wide spectrum of possibilities exists, from warm sunny days to fresh snow on the peak. It is not unusual for the summit's upper slopes to receive fresh snow or measurable amounts of hail, sleet, and rain during the summer. Plan for the worst by bringing the proper clothing for freezing temperatures, wind, rain, snow, hail, and sleet on the upper slopes.

Skiing or snowboarding in the area during the winter and spring presents many more weather and safety hazards. Although the weather is excellent much of the time, a backcountry traveler must be prepared for deep snow, strong winds, snowstorms, blizzards, avalanches, whiteouts, and temperatures to zero degrees Fahrenheit. For a complete discussion of winter and early spring snow conditions, see my book *50 Classic Backcountry Ski and Snowboard Summits in California: Mount Shasta to Mount Whitney*. This ski mountaineering guide details ski and snowboard routes on 50 backcountry summits (including Whitney) and provides a comprehensive discussion of winter weather, snow conditions, avalanche safety, equipment, clothing, and much more.

HYPOTHERMIA

A primary concern during the summer is afternoon thunderstorms. Without the proper clothing, such wet and windy conditions can quickly lead to hypothermia. Hypothermia can be a potentially serious medical problem in the mountains, especially above the tree line. If a hiker becomes wet, the wind can quickly strip the body of its core heat. A low windspeed of 10 to 20 miles per hour can have a dramatic and potentially fatal effect on a wet hiker. Furthermore, hypothermia often occurs at ambient air temperatures above freezing. The best prevention is not to get wet in the first place by taking windproof and water-repellent outer clothing such as a poncho, parka, or other water-protective garments.

The symptoms of hypothermia are decreased mental acuity, reduced physical ability, slowness, tiredness, confusion, and, after shivering has ceased, coma and death. A hiker or climber is at risk for hypothermia when wet and tired. Moisture on one's skin or clothing is the enemy. Wet falling snow, sleet, hail, or rain from a summer thunderstorm can quickly soak a hiker. If not adequately protected against these elements, a cold, wet, and tired hiker can quickly develop hypothermia.

Hypothermia is a condition in which the core body temperature decreases to a level at which normal muscular and cerebral functions are impaired. Normal body temperature is within ±1 degree of 98.6 degrees Fahrenheit. As the core body temperature drops, various symptoms of hypothermia appear. At core body temperatures between 93 and 96 degrees Fahrenheit, muscular incoordination, weakness, a slow, stumbling pace, mild confusion, and apathy appear. As the core body temperature drops further there is gross muscle incoordination, frequent stumbling, and mental sluggishness, with slow thought and speech. Hallucinations may develop. Shivering often is uncontrollable. At lower body temperatures, between 78 and 82 degrees Fahrenheit, cerebral function deteriorates, and death results from cessation of effective heart function.

Effective water- and wind-resistant clothing for your head, hands, body, and feet is critical. Compounding the environmental factors is moisture from perspiration. Whether your clothing gets wet from precipitation or perspiration, the result is the same: risk of hypothermia. Keep yourself and your clothing dry at all times. Use the layering method: a synthetic wicking layer next to the skin, a layer such as pile or fleece for insulation, and a breathable waterproof layer on the exterior. Remove or add layers as conditions dictate. Keeping well nourished and hydrated helps maintain normal body temperature.

Do not hike alone. A hypothermic person quickly loses the ability to think rationally and will not take the necessary actions to save his or her life. A partner is invaluable in recognizing the early danger signs of hypothermia and can take the critical life-saving action.

Upon detecting sings of hypothermia, seek shelter immediately to stop further heat loss. Place the victim inside a tent or hut so that he or she is protected from the wind, cold, and precipitation. Replace the victim's wet clothing with dry clothing and place him or her in a sleeping bag. Provide warm fluids immediately. Avoid caffeinated drinks because they act as a diuretic and contribute to volume depletion (loss of body fluids through urination). Previously experts advised sharing body heat through body-to-body contact in a sleeping bag. However, surface rewarming (e.g., body-to-body contact, hot water bottles to the skin) suppresses shivering, which is believed to be the safest method of rewarming the body core. If the hypothermia appears to be severe, rapidly plan a rescue. For further reading on field management of hypothermia, see *Backcountry Medical Guide* by Peter Steele, M.D.

MOUNTAIN SICKNESS

In addition to hypothermia, another concern for those hiking Mount Whitney is mountain sickness (altitude sickness). Mountain sickness undoubtedly stops more people from summiting than any other factor. Reviewing the most recent records of the 30,000 people who received permits, two out of every three failed to reach the summit. This rate of failure is high for a mountain with excellent trails to the top. This high failure rate can be attributed to three primary reasons: poor planning, inadequate conditioning, and mountain sickness. The deck is stacked against a poorly prepared hiker who drives from near sea level to 8300 feet at the Whitney Portal, 10,000 feet at Horseshoe Meadow, or 9200 feet at Onion Valley trailhead and immediately begins to hike. Many arrive at camp that first night with a splitting headache, feeling nauseous, dizzy, with no energy or desire to continue.

Mountain sickness is caused by hypobaric hypoxia (reduced atmospheric pressure due to increased altitude, which results in the lack of oxygen available to the body). Typically symptoms are not noted until 8000 to 10,000 feet has been attained, with about 10 to 40 percent of hikers experiencing symptoms. At 14,000 feet a hiker can perform only about 60 percent of his or her normal sea level capacity. Because the air is thinner at elevation, each breath contains much less oxygen. Therefore, less oxygen reaches the brain, internal organs, tissues, and muscles. The mechanism by which the reduced oxygen level produces the various symptoms of mountain sickness is uncertain, but the evidence suggests some alteration in the cells lining the small blood vessels that allows water to leave the blood vessels and accumulate in the tissues in an abnormal manner.

Mountain sickness is a continuum of increasing severity and consequences. What begins as a mild problem may progress into something much worse. Although individual susceptibility to mountain sickness is highly variable, hikers who have already had one or more episodes, young children, and women in the premenstrual phase are at highest risk.

Mountain sickness is not a specific disease but a group of widely varying symptoms caused by a rapid rise in elevation, including acute mountain sickness (AMS), generalized edema, disordered sleep, high-altitude pulmonary edema (HAPE), and high-altitude cerebral edema (HACE). These disorders represent a spectrum of altitude-related problems from the less serious AMS to the often fatal HAPE or HACE.

Acute Mountain Sickness

Symptoms of mild AMS are similar to those of a hangover or the flu: lack of energy, loss of appetite, mild headache, nausea, dizziness, shortness of breath, general feeling of lassitude, and disturbed sleep. These symptoms generally resolve over 24 to 48 hours at a given altitude and resolve more quickly if one descends. Acetazolamide (a mild diuretic that acidifies the blood) 125 mg taken twice a day may be used by those who suffer repeatedly from unpleasant symptoms despite a slow ascent. This prescription medication should be taken only until maximum altitude is attained or for 2 days, whichever is less. It will lessen your chances of getting AMS by about 30 to 50 percent. Side effects include a tingling of the face and fingers and frequent urination. Victims experiencing moderate mountain sickness involving severe headache, nausea, and vomiting must descend immediately.

Children are more prone to AMS than are adults. It is best to take children on hikes to several lower peaks in the 11,000- to 13,000-foot range to see how they perform at these elevations before planning a trip to Whitney. When attempting Whitney with children, plan several extra days for additional acclimatization. A slower rate of ascent decreases the incidence of AMS in children and adults alike and improves a party's chances for success.

General Edema

General edema is a harmless disorder occurring during the first couple of days to a week at high altitude. Edema is an abnormal collection of fluid in the extracellular, extravascular compartment, typically in dependent parts of the extremities. Edema probably is caused by the increased permeability of small blood vessels and reduced kidney function resulting from reduced oxygen concentrations in the blood. This fluid retention can cause a noticeable weight gain of 4 or more pounds. The excess fluid retention can cause a swelling of the face, eyelids, ankles, feet, fingers, and hands. Urine output may be scanty despite adequate fluid intake. In the absence of AMS, edema can be treated effectively with a diuretic.

Disordered Sleep

Disordered sleep is as troublesome to the person experiencing the symptoms as it is to his or her tent mate. The symptoms include fitful sleep, Cheyne–Stokes respirations (periods of not breathing for up to 60 seconds followed by rapid breathing while asleep), and a sense of general tiredness the next morning. In some hikers, it is the only symptom of high altitude, and it may persist the entire time while at elevation. Presumably, the mechanism causing disordered sleep is cerebral hypoxia. Acetazolamide (125 mg) taken before going to sleep may help to reduce the symptoms.

High-Altitude Pulmonary Edema

A much more serious form of mountain sickness is HAPE. Symptoms are inordinate shortness of breath and a dry, nonproductive cough or a cough producing a small amount of pink-tinged sputum (caused by blood from the lungs). HAPE results in a filling of the lung's air sacs with fluid that has oozed through the walls of the pulmonary capillaries. As more air sacs are filled with fluid, the oxygen

The north face of Mount Whitney and Sierra Richins from the summit of Mount Russell (Routes 4 and 5)

transfer to the pulmonary capillaries is blocked, resulting in cyanosis (decreased oxygen saturation of hemoglobin, with a bluish cast to the lips and nail beds). Without immediate treatment, HAPE may eventually lead to severe hypoxia, coma, and death. Treatment is immediate descent. If descent is not possible, supplemental oxygen administered at a rate of 4–6 liters per minute may be helpful along with nifedipine (20 mg, slow release, given every 6 hours).

High-Altitude Cerebral Edema

Another serious form of mountain sickness is HACE. It is characterized by severe headache, nausea, vomiting, mental confusion, poor judgment, ataxia (clumsy or uncoordinated gait), and eventually coma and death. In the case of HACE, fluid is retained in the brain cavity, causing swelling inside the skull. Both HAPE and HACE are rare in the Sierra Nevada, occurring in only about 0.5 percent and 0.1 percent of hikers respectively, in hikers venturing above 8500 feet. Both HAPE and HACE are true emergencies necessitating immediate descent and immediate medical attention. Lowering a climber 1000 to 3000 feet often can make a significant difference. If descent is not possible, administer supplemental oxygen at a rate of 4–6 liters per minute and dexamethazone (4 mg, given orally, intramuscularly, or intravenously every 6 hours). These treatments can be helpful, but their administration should not delay descent.

Prevention and Recovery

There are several things you can do to prevent or reduce the severity of mountain sickness. The most important is to take your time ascending the mountain. It is helpful to camp at the end of the road or as high as possible for one or two nights before beginning your hike. This will help your body adjust to the higher altitude. Spending at least two nights above 11,000 feet on your way to the summit is extremely helpful.

Drink plenty of water or your favorite sport drink. Research suggests that there is a direct correlation between fluid intake and susceptibility to altitude sickness. Ample fluid intake is essential to preventing dehydration and altitude sickness.

The following measures will help alleviate the discomfort associated with mountain sickness and may promote recovery.

▲ Avoid heavy exertion but maintain light activity (such as walking) to increase circulation. The natural tendency is to lie down and rest, but this reduces circulation.

▲ Drink plenty of water, more than you think is necessary. A sport drink also is beneficial.

▲ Eat light meals, avoiding too much fat. Warm soups are excellent.

▲ Take an aspirin, acetaminophen, or ibuprofen for symptom relief.

▲ Monitor closely for HAPE or HACE. If early signs are apparent the victim must be taken 2000–3000 feet lower. If an immediate improvement is not observed, remove the victim from the mountain.

DEHYDRATION AND WATER PURIFICATION

Losses of 2–4 liters of liquid per day from perspiration, breathing, and urination are common for backcountry hikers. Dehydration is further compounded by the symptoms of mountain sickness: nausea, vomiting, and a dulling of the thirst sensation that accompanies a loss of appetite. Studies suggest that dehydration contributes to depression, impaired judgment, and other psychological changes that occur at high altitudes.

Inadequate fluid replacement results in reduced circulating blood volume, the symptoms of which are decreased work capacity, feelings of exhaustion, and ultimately dizziness. The water you are carrying should be conveniently available. Water that is easily accessible is more readily used. Drink small amounts of water often. Supplementing the water with an electrolyte sport drink helps replace daily fluid losses. Soup with breakfast and dinner also aids with water and mineral repletion. Thirst often is not an accurate indication of your fluid needs. Therefore, drink more fluids than you think are necessary throughout the day to prevent dehydration.

The lack of safe drinking water is another factor contributing to dehydration. Because of the large number of hikers using the trails and the associated problems of sanitation, it is unsafe to drink untreated water. In addition to the large number of hikers in the area, native and nonnative animals can be carriers of *Giardia lamblia*.

One of the most bothersome and potentially debilitating illnesses in the backcountry is gastrointestinal (GI) illness. GI illness results in diarrhea, and *Giardia lamblia* is its most common cause in the mountains of California. Water taken from streams must be assumed to carry *Giardia lamblia,* a waterborne protozoan infectious diarrheal agent. Severe diarrhea, abdominal cramps, and sometimes vomiting are the symptoms of *Giardia lamblia* infection. Water loss through diarrhea can be debilitating. Treatment is metronidazole (250 mg) taken orally three times a day for 5 days.

FACT SHEET ON GIARDIASIS

Giardiasis is an infection caused by the intestinal parasite *Giardia lamblia,* which may or may not cause symptoms. The parasite survives outside the body as a cyst. When swallowed, it changes into an active form (trophozoite), multiplying and feeding in the upper intestine.

Those at risk: People of all ages.

Incubation period: 7–21 days (rarely shorter) after exposure to the parasite.

Exposure sources: Drinking water that has been contaminated by human or animal feces (even "clear" mountain water from streams, lakes, and springs may be contaminated).

Prevention: Treat all water sources. Effective water purification methods to prevent giardiasis include iodine tablets, filtering, and boiling.

Severity: Giardiasis can make you very sick but it is not usually life-threatening. Fortunately, it does not spread beyond the gastrointestinal tract.

Symptoms: If symptoms occur, they may include

▲ Diarrhea or loose stools, usually foul smelling and greasy

▲ If giardiasis lasts more than 5 days, diarrhea may alternate with constipation

▲ High abdominal cramps

▲ Bloating, gas, and belching

▲ Loss of appetite and weight loss

▲ Nausea and vomiting

▲ Dehydration

▲ Low-grade fever (usually)

Duration: A few days to several months.

Treatment: Metronidazole 250 mg taken orally three times a day for 5 days.

There are three acceptable methods for treating the water: iodine tablets, filtering, and boiling. All are effective against *Giardia*.

Medical research has established that iodine tablets are a highly effective agent for sterilizing drinking water. In extremely cold water, allow 10–30 minutes for the tablets to dissolve. To speed the process, break the tablet into small pieces as you add it to the water. If you do not like the flavor left by the iodine tablet, you can buy a neutralizing tablet that eliminates the offending taste. A sport drink also masks the iodine flavor effectively. Iodine also is effective at killing water-borne viruses. Iodine tablets are the least costly way to treat drinking water, and their weight is negligible.

Water filters are a reasonable method to purify water, but they have one serious drawback: they do not remove waterborne viruses. Viral contamination of the backcountry is not common, but viral diseases such as hepatitis are quite serious. Filtering alone does not ensure safe drinking water. Other disadvantages of water filters are their cost, the added weight in one's backpack, and the time and effort it takes to pump and filter the water.

Boiling water for 3 minutes kills most infectious microorganisms, including *Giardia* cysts. Boiling the water is a highly effective way to ensure safe drinking water, but it is inconvenient and time-consuming.

SUNBURN AND SNOW BLINDNESS

Sunburn is more easily prevented than treated. Apply sunblock lotion frequently and generously during the day. Use a sunblock that provides the greatest amount of protection (SPF 40 or greater), which protects against both ultraviolet A and B rays. Sunblock in conjunction with a wide-brimmed hat and fabric that hangs around the neck and face is most effective in preventing sunburn to the face and neck. Apply aloe vera gel to sunburned and wind-chapped skin to promote healing.

Snow blindness is a potential problem whenever large amounts of snow remain on the ground. In the simplest terms, snow blindness is sunburn of the epithelial layer (cornea) of the eye. Ultraviolet rays are present and threatening in any weather condition during the day. To protect against the damaging affects of the ultraviolet rays, it is essential to wear sunglasses at all times when traveling on snow. Even when it is cloudy and snowing, snow blindness can occur after only a few hours of unprotected exposure. Additionally, even when snow is not present it is a good practice to wear sunglasses when hiking at higher elevations because there is significantly less atmosphere to filter the effects of ultraviolet rays. Snow blindness is extremely painful because the eyelid moves over the inflamed cornea. Treatment is an eye patch over the affected eye for 24–48 hours. In most cases, the eyes heal quickly.

ACHES AND PAINS

You will experience aches, pains, and sore muscles and joints during and after your hike. Ibuprofen and naproxen are the wonder drugs for hikers and climbers. Taken with food once or twice during the day, these over-the-counter miracle drugs help ease the aches, pains, and soreness associated with strenuous climbing and hiking. A tablet at midday acts as a powerful second wind for the tired and sore hiker. Another tablet taken before bed helps reduce stiffness and greatly improves the quality of sleep. Five to ten minutes of stretching exercises at the end of the hike as part of the cooling-down process, and then again before bedtime, is also extremely helpful in reducing stiffness and improving sleep.

LIGHTNING

The first fatality from a lightning bolt was recorded on July 26, 1904, when a member of a scientific party was struck and killed on the summit of Whitney. More recently, a climber was killed by a lightning strike as he sought shelter in the stone hut on the summit. The summit hut has since been grounded but is still considered unsafe during a lightning storm.

Although it is not one of the main concerns of hikers on Mount Whitney, lightning has caused a number of serious (and mostly avoidable) accidents and should be taken seriously when thunderheads form over the Sierra Nevada (primarily in July and August). The very nature of ascending the peak places hikers and climbers in vulnerable spots that are the most frequent targets of lightning: high and exposed peaks and ridges. Peaks and ridges help produce the vertical updrafts and thundercloud conditions that generate lightning.

There are three types of lightning hazard: a direct strike, ground currents, and induced currents (in the immediate vicinity of a strike). Lightning is electricity, and when the more than 100 billion billion electrons in an average bolt strike a peak or tree, they spread instantaneously in all directions. The electrical discharge radiates outward and downward, decreasing rapidly as the distance from the strike increases.

Two factors determine the extent of injury to hikers and climbers: the amount of current received and the part of the body affected. The most serious threat is current running from one hand to the

Hiking the Mount Whitney Trail (Route 6)

other, passing through the heart and lungs, or from head to foot, passing through the vital organs. This is serious even if the amount of current is small. A hiker can survive a larger amount of current if it does not pass through vital organs.

The first rule is to avoid areas that might be hit by lightning. Seek a location with nearby projections or masses that are significantly higher and closer than one's head to any clouds. In a forest, the best place is among the shorter trees. Along a ridge the best location is in the middle because the ends are more exposed and susceptible to strikes. The following are some useful tips for hikers caught in a lightning storm:

▲ If a lightning storm is approaching, descend quickly to a safe location away from the summit and off exposed ridges.

▲ If caught unexpectedly by a lightning storm in an exposed position, seek a location with nearby projections or masses that are significantly higher than your head.

▲ Avoid moist areas, including crevices and gullies.

▲ Sit, crouch, or stand on an insulating object such as a coiled rope, sleeping bag, or sleeping pad.

▲ Occupy as small an area as possible. Keep your feet close together and hands off the ground.

▲ Stay out of small depressions; choose instead a narrow, slight rise to avoid ground currents. A small detached rock on a scree slope is excellent.

▲ Stay away from overhangs and out of small caves.

▲ When on a ledge, crouch at the outer edge, at least 4 feet from the rock wall.

BEARS AND OTHER MISCHIEVOUS CRITTERS

Adult black bears roaming the Sierra Nevada and other parts of California weigh up to 350 pounds and come in many shades of brown, black, and cinnamon. Generally, they are not as dangerous or as aggressive as the grizzly bear, but they can inflict serious damage on parked cars (in search of stored food) and can devour a week's supply of food in a matter of minutes.

When bears repeatedly raid campsites and garbage cans, these intelligent animals quickly learn that human food is much easier to obtain and tastier than their natural diet. Once they taste our food they begin to crave it and in the process become less fearful. A fearless bear may become destructive and dangerous. To help avoid this problem, proper food storage is required by federal regulations and feeding wildlife is prohibited. Violations can result in a hefty fine.

Bears are an ever-present problem at certain trailhead parking lots, campgrounds, and backcountry campsites. Many have become adept at breaking into parked cars and bringing down bear bags hung from tree limbs. Do not leave food, toiletries, sunscreen, soap, garbage, empty ice chests, or anything with a smell in a parked car. Bears have learned to recognize the shape of ice chests and have broken into cars for empty ice chests. Any empty ice chest left in a parked car should be concealed.

Bears in some wilderness locations have become overly friendly and will approach a campsite in the daytime. Use the wilderness bear-proof food storage boxes placed by the National Park Service. Do not leave food, toothpaste, soap, or any item with an odor in your tent. When wilderness bear-proof food storage boxes or portable bear-proof canisters are not available, use the counterbalance method to hang food and other items from a tree limb. The counterbalance method can be effective, if done correctly, but many bears have been successful in outsmarting many elaborate methods hikers have used to hang their food. The Forest Service and National Park Service are now requiring

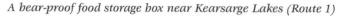

A bear-proof food storage box near Kearsarge Lakes (Route 1)

hikers to take plastic bear-proof canisters with them into certain locations in the backcountry. Check with the Forest Service or National Park Service to determine which areas require these bear-proof containers. Portable bear-proof canisters are available for rent or purchase at the Lodgepole and Cedar Grove Visitor Centers, Mineral King Ranger Station, Whitney Portal Store, and some Forest Service ranger stations.

The National Park Service has placed bear-proof food storage boxes at selected wilderness locations that are notorious for hungry bear activity. Nearly forty bear-proof food storage boxes have been placed in twenty-five Sequoia and Kings Canyon National Parks wilderness locations along Routes 1–3 and 8–13. Most of these wilderness-placed food storage boxes are approximately 48 x 18 x 18 inches. At Kearsarge Lakes and other heavily used locations, larger boxes have been placed measuring approximately 48 x 24 x 30 inches. Routes 4–7 do not have bear-proof food storage boxes because these trails are ostensibly located in Forest Service wilderness areas. For some reason the Forest Service has not followed the lead of the National Park Service in placing bear-proof food storage boxes in the backcountry. Box locations are described in Chapters 5 and 6 under the route descriptions and are noted on the maps.

Marmots, chipmunks, mice, blue jays, ravens, and other small, mischievous critters can also feast on a backpacker's food if it is not properly protected. When hanging food to protect against marmots and chipmunks, also keep in mind blue jays and ravens. A hanging food bag may be an open invitation to lunch for our flying friends.

Certain trailhead parking areas, especially at Mineral King (Routes 12 and 13), are plagued by marmots. Marmots have been known to damage cars by climbing into the engine compartment and eating hoses and wires. If you park your car for any length of time where there is a history of marmot problems, consider placing chicken wire or a mesh completely around it to keep the marmots out. Ask the Forest Service or National Park Service for information on trailhead conditions and advice about marmot damage to parked cars.

Mosquitoes, biting midges, and gnats can be a problem early in the hiking season near meadows and along creeks, or anywhere standing water exists. Mosquitoes are not a serious problem in June and July but are bothersome enough to merit taking a mosquito repellent. Sunscreen with an added mosquito repellent is quite effective. By August and September the problem resolves itself.

▲ Chapter 3 ▲
What to Take

Selecting the correct gear, clothing, footwear, equipment, and food is critical in attaining the freedom of the hills necessary for a safe and successful trip. Just as importantly, this chapter explains how to keep the weight of your pack to a minimum without sacrificing comfort at camp and safety in the backcountry.

The authors of *Mountaineering: The Freedom of the Hills* state that a mountaineer is one who seeks the freedom of the hills, full wilderness citizenship, with no barriers he or she cannot pass, no dangers he or she cannot avoid. Freedom of the hills lies largely in the ability to cope with every problem of travel and living and every emergency with nothing more than what a party can carry conveniently on its shoulders. Equipment must be kept to the safe minimum, with no frills and luxuries, and must be as lightweight as is consistent with durability and versatility.

Maximize your enjoyment in the wilderness by going light. Many hikers, even the experienced, take too much with them. You can get by with a lot less than you think without sacrificing safety. Speed in the mountains means safety and enjoyment. It is difficult to move through the mountains quickly with an oversized pack, weighing 40 or 50 pounds, stuffed to the brim with the latest gadgets from your favorite mountaineering store. When considering purchasing items, whether hiking boots, a parka, pack, sleeping bag, or tent, think function and weight. The weight of each item you take is critical because you must carry all of it. If a week's worth of supplies do not fit inside a 4000-cubic-inch (60- to 70-liter) internal frame pack, you are taking too much.

Appendix 2 includes two equipment checklists, one for an overnight trip for backpackers and the second for a single-day hike. Photocopy the lists and use them. They will serve as a convenient reminder and quick check against accidentally leaving a critical item at home.

CLOTHING AND GEAR

The following is a discussion of some of the more important gear and clothing items necessary for a successful ascent of the peak. This section, as well as the Appendix 2 equipment checklists, assumes a trip during June through October. Additional equipment and warmer clothes are needed for other times of the year. For a discussion of winter conditions on Mount Whitney and route descriptions, review *50 Classic Backcountry Ski and Snowboard Summits in California: Mount Shasta to Mount Whitney*.

Footwear

If you are planning a single-day hike via the Mount Whitney Trail, select the most comfortable pair of trail hiking shoes or light- to medium-weight hiking boot you own. The most important criteria are comfort and footbed support. Hiking 22 miles in a single day can be grueling on the feet and legs. For a multiday trip, select a comfortable, supportive, light- to medium-weight hiking boot. Because you will be carrying a pack, additional foot support, ankle support, and traction are desirable. For one of the cross-country routes in the guidebook, select a sturdy, medium-weight boot. Generally, trail hiking shoes are not adequate for cross-country travel because they do not provide the desired support and ankle protection, and because of their low cut they fill easily with loose scree.

Trail hiking shoes and light hiking boots have been upgraded significantly in recent years. When purchasing a pair of trail hiking shoes or light hiking boots, select one with torsional rigidity. Take the shoe or boot in your hands and attempt to twist the sole as if wringing out a wet washrag. The sole and footbed should offer considerable resistance. If you can twist the sole easily, do not purchase the shoe or boot. This torsional rigidity provides increased arch support, protection, and comfort on long hikes and helps with edging on steep scree slopes and on snow.

Socks

Do not use cotton socks or socks with a high percentage of nylon or polyester fibers. Your feet will sweat profusely and your socks will be soaked by the end of the day. Rather, use medium-weight socks containing a high percentage of wool. One normally thinks of wool socks for the warmth they provide in the winter, but wool is the best choice, even in summer. Bring an extra pair and rotate socks each day.

Parka or Poncho

The weather is unpredictable. Thundershowers accompanied by winds are common on summer afternoons. Prepare for this eventuality by taking a weatherproof parka or rain poncho. Several large garbage bags can help in an emergency, but they tear easily and are not effective in high winds. Lightweight nylon wind pants also are desirable to protect against strong winds.

Clothing

The weather and temperature can change rapidly. For this reason, one must plan for the worst by being prepared with the proper clothing for freezing temperatures above 11,000 feet, with the potential for wind, rain, snow, and sleet. In these conditions, synthetic fibers are desirable. Do not wear cotton clothing because it soaks up moisture, is slow to dry, and provides little warmth when wet.

The following is an example of the clothing necessary during the summer and early fall. Wear a midweight, long-sleeve polypropylene top next to your skin, followed by a light powerstretch or microfleece vest. In colder weather, add a 200-weight fleece jacket with a hood and a water-repellent and windproof parka with a hood.

For the bottom half, two layers usually are adequate. Make the first layer midweight, polypropylene bottoms with baggy nylon shorts worn over them. When the weather turns cold or the wind picks up, add the second layer, a pair of wind pants with full-length zippers. The beauty of this layering system is that in warm weather you can wear the shorts alone. If the temperature drops suddenly, slip on the nylon wind pants over the shorts. On colder mornings, start with the polypropylene bottoms and the shorts, followed by the wind pants.

Tents

Balancing the weight, function, and size of a tent is difficult. Expedition-grade and four-season tents provide ample protection but tend to be

Sunrise at camp near Upper Boy Scout Lake (Routes 4 and 5)

much too heavy. Three-season tents are lighter and provide adequate protection depending on the quality of the tent. Unfortunately, many two-person tents are small and cramped for two.

Most three- and four-season tents weigh 7 pounds or more. This is too much. You will be carrying the tent on your back for many hours. Look for freestanding tents in the 5- to 6-pound range. When comparing tent weights, take an accurate scale with you to the store and weigh the tents you are considering. The challenge for the shopper is to find a tent that is roomy, sturdy, lightweight, and economical. There are a few on the market, but improvements are needed. The task for the tent designers is to reduce the weight of their tents while increasing the inside volume for the shoulders and head area.

Sleeping Bags

A down sleeping bag rated to about 20 or 25 degrees Fahrenheit is an excellent choice. A synthetic-filled bag is also a good choice because it is less expensive, but it is heavier and does not compress as neatly as down. Use a closed-cell or self-inflating sleeping pad. A self-inflating sleeping pad is more comfortable but it is also the more expensive choice.

Backpacks

An internal frame pack is preferred. An internal frame pack holds the load close to the back. This reduces the tendency of the pack to shift on uneven or steep terrain, thereby throwing the hiker off balance. If hiking is limited to trails with little or no cross-country travel, an external frame pack also is a good choice.

Today's packs are far superior to the packs of yesteryear. However, design improvements are sorely needed. Today's internal frame packs are overbuilt and much too heavy. Packs weighing 6, 7, and 8 pounds don't merit your consideration. Find a pack that weighs less than 5 pounds. A 5-pound pack with a 2.5-pound sleeping bag weighs less than many of the overbuilt packs on the market. When shopping for a backpack, take an accurate scale with you to compare weights.

Crampons and Ice Ax

Crampons and ice ax usually are not needed to summit Mount Whitney. However, there are two exceptions. You should bring them when climbing the Mountaineers Route (Route 5) any time during the year and when hiking any of the trails in the spring season (May and June) when there is snow on the upper slopes of the mountain. These tools can increase your danger unless you are skilled in their use. Instruction by a qualified climber/instructor with practice in the field will help, but merely reading about crampons and ice axes in a book invites a false sense of security. Check with the appropriate backcountry rangers for trail conditions.

Stoves

There are many excellent, lightweight backpacking stoves on the market today. All perform adequately. My favorite style is a hanging stove. Designed to hang inside your tent, it allows you to cook in the tent when cold and windy weather persists or in the early morning, when it is still dark outside. Early in the morning, when it is freezing outside, or at night after a long and tiring day, it is convenient to cook a meal while relaxing in the warmth of your tent and sleeping bag. Make sure the tent is adequately vented and use caution when lighting the stove.

Cooking Pot and Bowl

Take a single 1- to 1.5-quart cooking pot. A single cooking pot is all you need to prepare the meals suggested in the Menu Planner in Appendix 4. For eating utensils, take a 2-cup plastic measuring cup and a plastic spoon. This is all you need.

First-Aid Kit

The contents of a wilderness first-aid kit are included in Appendix 3.

ALPINE CUISINE: SOME TASTY SUGGESTIONS

Good food gives a festive touch to summit successes and lifts the spirits during stormy days. Good food improves the scenery and keeps the spirits high. Bad food makes the nights colder, the approaches more difficult, the weather unbearable, and good friends intolerable. The key to good food is finding cuisine that you like and look forward to eating. At altitude this is not always easy.

Adequate food and liquid intake is extremely important. Many hikers experience a lack of appetite when going to higher elevations. Others may be too tired at the end of a hard day to be interested in food. Resist the temptation to skip a meal. Eating is essential for the sustained effort needed in the backcountry. Much of the physical fatigue and weakness experienced at high altitudes are caused by inadequate food intake, dehydration, and possibly potassium loss.

To keep adequately nourished and maintain the high levels of caloric intake necessary for hiking at altitude, snack often and eat small portions regularly. Select good food, fun food, food that you enjoy at home. If you don't like a food item at home, you will hate it at elevation. Avoid fatty foods and foods that are difficult to digest. Sweets are easily digested and are craved, even at altitude, by most hikers. Soups are easily prepared and easy to eat and should be enjoyed by all. Eat light and eat often.

Studies indicate that balancing one's protein and carbohydrate intake can improve performance. However, in the mountains it is difficult to plan an adequately balanced diet of protein and carbohydrates because carbohydrates usually dominate, from bagels to pasta to power bars. Some suggestions for protein sources include turkey and beef jerky; canned salmon, tuna, and chicken; protein powder added to hot cereal; cheese and cream cheese; peanut butter; mixed nuts; and nutrition bars that balance protein and carbohydrates. All are excellent protein choices for your mountain menu.

The Menu Planner in Appendix 4 suggests breakfast, lunch, and dinner menus that are simple to prepare, inexpensive, and lightweight and are superior to the freeze-dried meals sold in backpacking stores. You can buy all suggested food items at your local grocery store, and you will need minimal cooking equipment to prepare them. The suggested cuisine also attempts to strike a reasonable balance between carbohydrate and protein intake. For further reading, a number of excellent outdoor cookbooks are available, such as *Backcountry Cooking: From Pack to Plate in 10 Minutes,* by Dorcas S. Miller, and *Gorp, Glop & Glue Stew: Favorite Foods from 165 Outdoor Experts,* by Yvonne Prater and Ruth Dyar Mendenhall.

Drink plenty of fluids. Throughout the day, keep hydrated by drinking water or a sport drink regularly. Again, at dinner, drink plenty of sport drinks or water along with a hot drink and plenty of hot soup.

As a general rule, plan 2 pounds of food per person per day. The Menu Planner in Appendix 4 includes weights of each item. Adjust the portions based on the appetites of those in your party. Throw in a couple of extra soups for emergency rations.

▲ Chapter 4 ▲

Before Setting Out

Rise early. Fix a time-table to which you must try to keep. One seldom regrets having made an early start, but one always regrets having set off too late; first for reasons of safety — the adage 'it is later than you think' is very true in the mountains — but also because of the strange beauty of the moment: the day comes to replace the night, the peaks gradually lighten, it is the hour of mystery but also of hope. Setting off by lantern-light, witnessing the birth of a new day as one climbs to meet the sun, this is a wonderful experience.

Gaston Rébuffat, from *On Snow and Rock*

Before setting out for the summit, you must decide when to go and what route to take. Unfortunately, these choices may be determined by the availability of wilderness permits. Because of the high demand for permits to hike the Mount Whitney Trail, the Inyo National Forest has implemented a lottery system to award wilderness permits for this trail.

The good news is that a wilderness permit can be readily obtained for many other trails and cross-country routes. Selecting Route 2 (University Pass Route), Route 3 (Shepherd Pass Trail), and Route 7 (Meysan

Lake Route) almost guarantees you a wilderness permit. You can obtain permits almost as easily for Route 4 (Circumnavigation Route of Mount Whitney), Route 5 (Mountaineers Route), and the westside trails (Routes 10–13), especially if you select a midweek departure date. The most difficult trailheads to secure a permit for are the Mount Whitney Trail (Route 6), followed by Cottonwood Pass Trail (Route 9), New Army Pass Route (Route 8), and Kearsarge Pass Trail (Route 1). See "Wilderness Permits" below for details on securing permits.

If you cannot gain a wilderness permit through the lottery or secure a reservation for the other trails, a foolproof strategy will result in a permit: start your trip before the trail quotas are required. This strategy works best on Cottonwood Pass Trail (Route 9) because it is the first to open after the winter snows melt. For this trail, the wilderness trail quotas begin on the last Friday in June of each year. Start your trip before this date and return from Whitney over Cottonwood Pass or New Army Pass back to your starting point at Horseshoe Meadow Trailhead. If you plan to descend the Mount Whitney Trail, make sure your permit reflects this. Check with the Forest Service on the trail and snow conditions for both the Cottonwood Pass Trail and the Mount Whitney Trail. The end of June is an excellent time because the meadows are lush, the flowers in full bloom, and the creeks full of water from the spring melt. The trail along lower Rock Creek is especially enjoyable, and many deer browse in the vast meadows.

If you want a wilderness experience, do not hike the Mount Whitney Trail during the summer peak season but rather go in mid- to late October or select one of the other twelve trails and cross-country routes. Selecting one of these other routes increases your chance of securing a wilderness permit while allowing you to hike through some fantastic mountain terrain. Additionally, in the fall (mid-September through October) the crowds diminish on all the routes, including the Mount Whitney Trail. This is an excellent time to take your trip.

WHEN TO GO

The primary hiking season is June through September, with the most popular months being July and August. By mid-September, all the trails other than Route 6 see far fewer hikers.

There is no bad time to ascend the peak because all seasons have their unique characteristics that make a trip during that particular season a wonderfully rewarding experience. In the summer and fall, the Mount Whitney Trail and the Mountaineers Route (Route 5) can be hiked in a single day. The other trails and routes in this guidebook provide memorable multiday wilderness experiences. Whitney's east face includes spectacular technical climbing routes for the experienced rock climber. In the winter and spring, the area provides wonderful terrain for the ski mountaineer and backcountry snowboarder. In short, the mountain provides something for everyone year-round.

My favorite two seasons are fall and spring. A ski ascent of Mount Whitney in the spring (April and May) is an excellent way to experience the solitude and grandeur of the peak. Spring is when the winter snow turns to velvetlike spring corn, providing exquisite skiing and snowboarding. With 5 to 15 feet of snow covering the brush, boulders, talus, and steep couloirs, a ski mountaineer can proceed with confidence and freedom, without the geologic impediments experienced during the summer. The Mountaineers Route (Route 5) provides an exceptional ascent and descent route for the experienced ski mountaineer and snowboarder.

This being said, by far the best time for the hiker and backpacker to climb Whitney (by any route) is in the fall. Mid-September through October is a beautiful time for exploring the Sierra Nevada. The crowds are dwindling, the leaves of the quaking aspen trees are turning all shades of red and yellow, the mosquitoes and bugs are gone, the threat of afternoon thunderstorms has passed, and bear activity is on the decline. In the frosty fall mornings, skiffs of ice form on the lakes and streams but quickly melt in the morning sun. And in the evenings the crisp autumn air signals the rapid approach of winter. My annual fall trips into the Sierra Nevada have been some of the most enjoyable and memorable.

TRIP PLANNING TIPS

Regardless of the season selected, it is important to have a well-thought-out plan before setting out. Here are some tips to consider as you plan your trip.

▲ If you have not been to 14,000 feet before, take a preparatory trip ascending to 13,000 feet and camp above 11,000 feet. If you suffer no ill effects from the altitude, you should do well. However, if you experience altitude problems, plan several extra days to ascend Mount Whitney. Consider selecting a trail that takes at least 4 days to reach the summit, such as Routes 1, 3, 9, 10, 11, 12, or 13. The hike to the mountain will help you acclimatize to the elevation. If you must hike the Mount Whitney Trail (Route 6), spend two nights at Whitney Portal or Horseshoe Meadows Campground and plan two nights at Outpost Camp or Trail Camp before setting out for the summit.

▲ Establish a trip itinerary. Your itinerary should include a daily accounting of your plans, the name of the starting and ending trailheads, the trails you will use, planned campsite locations, and prominent peaks you will be climbing. Write down your trip itinerary and leave it with a responsible person. Also include a description of where you will park your vehicle; the make, model, year, and color of your vehicle; the license plate number; and your exit date from the mountains and the date you plan to return home.

▲ Secure a wilderness permit from the appropriate National Park Service or the National Forest District Office well in advance of your departure (see the discussion of wilderness permits in the next section).

▲ Study the map. Make sure all members of your party are familiar with the route.

▲ Make sure all members of your party are aware of the overall level of difficulty of the trip and the number of miles and elevation to be gained each day. The trip itinerary should not be too difficult for any member. If it is, select an alternative route or a less demanding itinerary. Your party is only as strong as the weakest member.

▲ If you take a GPS, ensure that you are fully versed in its use. Set the various coordinates of your route (e.g., starting point and end point, camps, lakes, passes, summits) before starting the trip.

▲ Complete an equipment check before departing. Ensure that all group items (e.g., tents, stoves, food) are accounted for and arrive at the trailhead.

▲ Don't go alone; hike with at least one other person.

WILDERNESS PERMITS

Wilderness permits are required year-round on all trails described in this guidebook. During the busy season these trailheads are also subject to wilderness quotas that limit the number of hikers allowed to enter the backcountry each day. You should make a wilderness permit reservation well in advance of your departure date for trips commencing during the quota season. For trips occurring outside the quota period, you can secure a permit the day of the trip at the issuing ranger station. The Inyo National Forest and the Sequoia and Kings Canyon National Parks have similar wilderness permit procedures, but there are enough differences to keep you on your toes. For Routes 1–9, look to the Inyo National Forest for your wilderness permit; for Routes 10–13, the permit is provided by the personnel of the Sequoia and Kings Canyon National Parks.

Although the National Park Service and the Forest Service believe that the details of their respective permit systems will be in place for many years to come, they are also open to suggestions and may make adjustments from time to time to improve service. Check with the Forest Service and National Park Service for current procedures.

Mount Whitney Zone

Because of the fragile alpine environment and the heavy use of the area, the Inyo National Forest and Sequoia and Kings Canyon National Parks have created a special designation called the Mount Whitney Zone. This 15-square-mile area surrounding the mountain was necessary to assist in the management and preservation of the area. This zone has special quotas for day hikers and backpackers. The quotas in this zone are in place from May 1 to November 1 of each year.

To effectively manage the number of hikers entering the Mount Whitney Zone, quotas have been placed on many trailheads even though they originate far from the peak. For example, the Kearsarge Pass Trail has an overall daily quota of sixty. However, the total number of hikers destined for Mount Whitney are limited by other quotas. Trails originating in Sequoia and Kings Canyon National Parks have an overall quota, just as the Forest Service trails do, but the Park Service does not place a secondary Mount Whitney Zone quota on their trailheads.

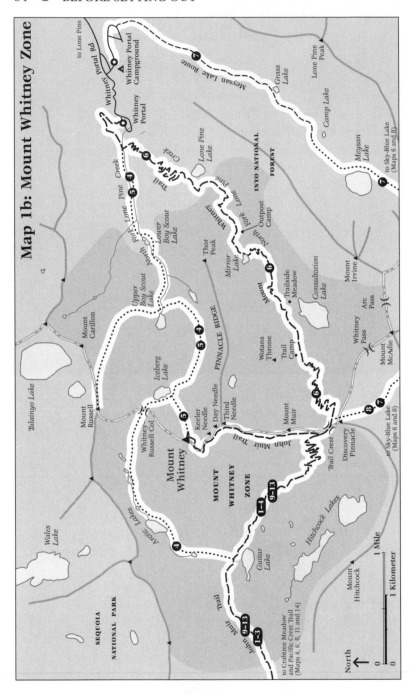

Map 1b: Mount Whitney Zone

Mount Whitney Trail (Route 6)

For the Mount Whitney Trail, wilderness permit quotas are in place from May 1 to November 1. A permit is required whether a single-day or a multiday trip is planned. Currently, a maximum of 150 day-use and 50 multiday hikers are allowed to begin their trips each day.

Mount Whitney Trail reservations are accepted during February. All requests for a permit, whether for day use or multiday use, postmarked in February, are placed in a lottery. Permit requests are randomly selected and processed one by one until permit space is no longer available for the entire quota season. If you are successful in securing a permit, it will be mailed to you. If not, your application and fee will be returned. To help defray the cost of the permit system and improve service to the public, a small fee is charged for each hiker and must accompany the reservation application.

It is expected that all dates will be completely booked through this process. However, if all permits are not allocated through the lottery, permit applications will be accepted. Cancellations and any unreserved dates are available on a first-come, first-served basis the day before or the day of departure.

Mountaineers Trail (Routes 4 and 5)

Routes 4 and 5 initially start up the Mount Whitney Trail but quickly leave the trail to ascend North Fork Lone Pine Creek via an unmaintained climber's trail. A day-use permit is not required for these routes. However, a permit for a multiday excursion is required. To secure advance reservations, send your request to the Forest Service up to six months in advance of your departure; these routes are not subject to the Mount Whitney Trail lottery. However, if you plan to ascend Route 5 (Mountaineers Route) and descend the Mount Whitney Trail, you must apply for a permit to enter the Mount Whitney Zone and use the Mount Whitney Trail.

All Other Trails Originating in the Inyo National Forest (Routes 1–3 and 7–9)

The U.S. Forest Service has used several different permit reservation systems in the past with varying degrees of success. Currently, approximately 60 percent of Inyo National Forest wilderness permits are available by reservation and 40 percent go to first-come, first-served walk-ins, except for the Mount Whitney Trail, where 100 percent are available through a lottery.

Wilderness permit reservations can be made up to six months prior to the departure date of your hike. On this date, mail or fax reservations for non–Mount Whitney Trail permits can be made. If making a reservation by mail, allow plenty of time for return confirmation of your permit by mail. Fax reservations can be made up to 24 hours before the trip. Wilderness permits not issued through this reservation process will be issued on a walk-in basis. Phone reservations may be available in the future. A small fee is charged for each reservation.

Permit requests are processed in order of the postmark or fax date. The more alternative dates listed on the application, the greater the probability of receiving a wilderness permit. Successful applicants are notified by mail with instructions for picking up the permit. If unsuccessful, the application and fee are returned.

The permit quota system is in place from May 1 to November 1 for these routes. The lone exception is Route 9. Its quotas run from the last Friday in June to September 15. Make sure you specify on your wilderness permit reservation application that you will be entering the Mount Whitney Zone and be sure to include the correct fee.

During February for the Mount Whitney Trail and up to six months in advance of your departure date for all other Inyo National Forest trails, mail, phone, or fax your wilderness permit application to:

Wilderness Reservation Office
Inyo National Forest
873 North Main Street
Bishop, CA 93514
Phone: 760-873-2483
Fax: 760-873-2484

Questions can be emailed through the website (www.r5.fs.fed.us/inyo), or call the Wilderness Information Line at 760-873-2485.

Unreserved, walk-up permits for Routes 1–9 can be secured at
Inyo National Forest
Mount Whitney Ranger Station
640 South Main Street
Lone Pine, CA 93545
Phone: 760-876-6200

At the trailhead for Meysan Lake (Route 7)

Trails Originating in the National Park (Routes 10–13)

For trails originating to the west of the Sierra Nevada crest (Routes 10–13), a wilderness permit is required from the Sequoia and Kings Canyon National Parks. Advance reservations are recommended (but not required) for all trips from May 21 through September 21. Wilderness permit advance reservations are highly recommended for trips starting during a holiday period or on a weekend. Trips starting in midweek are easier to secure.

Wilderness permit reservations can be made starting on March 1 of each year and can be made 21 days before the date of departure. The National Park Service Wilderness Office confirms permit reservations by mail. However, the actual wilderness permit must be picked up at the ranger station or visitor center near the trailhead by 9:00 A.M. the day of departure or the afternoon before. Reserved permits can be picked up at the Cedar Grove Visitor Center or Roads End for Route 10, at Lodgepole Visitor Center for Route 11, and at the Mineral King Ranger Station for Routes 12 and 13.

The *Sequoia Bark,* the free park newspaper, provides details on campgrounds, lodging, food, showers, and laundry. The park also produces *Backcountry Basics,* a useful newspaper-type publication detailing wilderness permit requirements, wilderness safety, trailheads, and the backcountry. To receive a copy of the *Sequoia Bark* or *Backcountry Basics,* contact any visitor center at the address and phone number listed in Appendix 5.

Each trail has a daily entry quota, of which approximately 66 percent are available for advance reservations. To make reservations for the routes originating in Sequoia and Kings Canyon National Parks, write or fax

Wilderness Permit Reservations
Sequoia and Kings Canyon National Parks
HCR 89 Box 60
Three Rivers, CA 93271
Phone: 559-565-3766 or 559-565-3341
Fax: 559-565-4239
Website: *www.nps.gov/seki*

First-come, first-served wilderness permits may be issued after 1:00 P.M. the afternoon before the trip or the morning of the trip. If the quota for the desired trail is full, you must choose another trail or another day to start. To avoid this unfortunate situation, make advance reservations. First-come, first-served wilderness permits are issued at a visitor center or ranger station near the trailhead: the Cedar Grove Visitor Center or Roads End Ranger Station for Route 10, the Lodgepole Visitor Center for Route 11, and the Mineral King Ranger Station for Routes 12 and 13.

Whether you request a wilderness permit reservation or secure a first-come, first-served permit, make sure that you request permission to enter the Mount Whitney Zone. Appendix 5 contains a list of useful wilderness permit contacts.

The crest of the Sierra Nevada serves as a natural boundary between the National Park Service and the U.S. Forest Service managed lands. To the west of the crest are the Sequoia and Kings Canyon National Parks and to the east are the wilderness areas managed by the U.S. Forest Service. Because the eastside trips begin in the National Forests and end in Sequoia National Park, you must follow the rules and regulations of both the Forest Service and the National Park Service. Three of the four westside routes (Routes 10–12) stay completely in Sequoia and Kings Canyon National Parks the entire distance, so their rules apply.

PROTECT THE FRAGILE ALPINE ECOLOGY

The Whitney area has become the most popular and heavily used area in the Sierra Nevada. With this popularity comes the added responsibility of those visiting the area to tread softly. We must all do our part to keep the area unspoiled. The following discussion contains a number of suggestions to help protect the fragile alpine ecology for the enjoyment of current and future generations.

Trail switchbacks are expensive to construct and maintain; shortcutting them causes erosion and damage. Please do not cut the switchbacks.

Avoid creating a new campsite; use established sites, never in meadows or on vegetation. Avoid camping under overhanging dead limbs or near leaning snags (dead trees). When possible, pick a site that is screened from the trail and other campers. Building campsite improvements such as rock walls, fire rings, tables, and chairs is prohibited.

Although most campsites are near water, select one at least 100 feet from streams and lakes. Many previously popular areas are closed to overnight camping; please honor these closures. Tread carefully and do not trample the small plants near your camp. Visualize potential impacts when selecting campsites, and leave flowers, rocks, and other natural features undisturbed.

Water pollution is one of the biggest problems in the Sierra Nevada. Mount Whitney is no exception because it is the most heavily used area in the Sierra Nevada, and the water quality in the region has suffered correspondingly. Treat all water before using (refer to Chapter 2 for a discussion of water purification methods).

There are two major causes of water contamination in the Whitney area: soap and human waste. Soap, even biodegradable soap, should not be used in the wilderness. It takes time to degrade and may be ingested by animals or humans before decomposing. If you must use even biodegradable soap, do not use it in or near streams and lakes. Pots and eating utensils can be cleaned with boiling water (and without soaps). Dispose of rinse water at least 100 feet from any water source because food particles can contaminate the water and promote algae growth.

Human waste is an even greater problem. The parasite *Giardia lamblia* originates from water and food contaminated by human and animal waste. Intestinal pathogens such as *Giardia lamblia* and *Escherichia coli* can live for many years in improperly buried waste. Use the established toilets where available. Solar toilets are located at Outpost Camp and Trail Camp (Route 6). A pit toilet is located on the summit, and several more have been strategically placed along some of the other high-use trails. If a toilet is not available, the best practice is to pack it out. This measure sounds extreme and is not yet required on Mount Whitney but is being implemented on other high-use areas such as Mount McKinley, Mount Rainier, and Mount Shasta. There is an experimental pack-it-out program for the North Fork Lone Pine Creek (Routes 4 and 5). Kits are available commercially and at the Lone Pine Ranger Station and include a seal-tight bag with a mixture similar to kitty litter to neutralize the odor.

The next best method to dispose of solid human waste is to dig a hole 8–10 inches deep and bury it. Make sure you are at least 200 feet from any water source. Pack out toilet paper, tampons, and sanitary napkins in plastic bags.

Proper food storage in bear territory is required by federal law. The Forest Service and National Park Service require backpackers to carry bear-proof canisters in some locations. Check with the appropriate forest or park ranger for current bear activity and the requirements for bear-proof containers. In the Sequoia National Park, bear-proof food boxes have been placed at certain locations. The specific locations of the wilderness bear-proof boxes are detailed in the route descriptions in Chapters 5 and 6. Where bear-proof boxes are not required, hang food out of reach of animals, at least 4 feet from the tree trunk and 10 feet from the ground.

Trash is another growing problem in the wilderness. Everything packed in must be packed out. Remove as much food packaging as possible at home before the trip to minimize the trash you need to pack out. Each member of your party should carry a small garbage bag or spare nylon stuff sack and be responsible for packing out his or her trash. A good wilderness citizen will also pick up and carry out additional trash found near campsites or along the trail. A goal of each wilderness traveler should be to leave the wilderness cleaner than when they arrived. If everyone made this a practice, great strides would be made in cleaning up the backcountry.

Campfires do not have a place in the backcountry. The scarce wood supply above 10,000 feet is not adequate to provide a sustainable source of wood for the thousands of hikers each year. In addition, the traditional rock fire ring is an environmental and ecological hazard. Generally speaking, the Forest Service and National Park Service have banned wood fires in the backcountry above 10,000 feet (the 10,000-foot elevation closure varies depending on specific site conditions). Wood fires should be limited to designated areas at trailhead campgrounds. Keep any fires small and consider using a

Kearsarge Lakes and Mount Brewer (prominent background peak), as seen from Kearsarge Pass (Route 1)

stove even where wood fires are permitted. Use only dead and down wood from outside the camp area.

In addition to the wilderness permit requirements discussed above, keep in mind the following general rules. Dogs and other pets are not allowed in Sequoia and Kings Canyon National Parks. The maximum group size is fifteen. Finally, firearms are not allowed in Sequoia and Kings Canyon National Parks. Discharging a firearm in the wilderness, outside the National Parks, is permitted only for hunting wildlife as allowed by state law.

TRAIL TIPS FOR A SINGLE-DAY ASCENT

Two routes in this guidebook, the Mount Whitney Trail (Route 6) and the Mountaineers Route (Route 5), lend themselves to a single-day ascent of the peak. Permits for 150 hikers a day are issued for the Mount Whitney Trail, and there are no single-day quotas for the Mountaineers Route. Many successfully hike the peak in a single day. Conversely, large numbers attempt the peak but fail to gain the summit because a single-day ascent is strenuous (22 miles round trip with more than 6000 feet of elevation gain). A single-day hike should be considered only by hikers in excellent physical condition. The following tips may increase the probability of success for those attempting a single-day ascent.

▲ If you have not been to 14,000 feet before, take a preparatory trip ascending to 13,000 feet and camp above 11,000 feet. If you suffer no ill effects from the altitude, you should do well.

▲ Sleep at an elevation above 8000 feet (or as high as possible) for at least one, preferably two nights immediately before your climb.

▲ Wear the most comfortable trail hiking shoes or light boots you own (see discussion in Chapter 3 on footwear).

▲ Take an extra pair of socks and change socks for the descent.

▲ Take moleskin and use it at the first hint of a hot spot to prevent a blister from forming.

▲ Get an early start (3:00 or 4:00 A.M). Many hikers take 12 to 18 hours to complete a round trip. If you leave promptly by 4:00 A.M., a 16-hour day will get you back to your car by 8:00 in the evening. A late start at 6:00 A.M. will put you back at the car at 10:00 at night.

▲ Take a flashlight or headlamp with extra batteries.

▲ Drink plenty of fluids the day before and throughout the day of the hike.

▲ Take 2 liters of water or sport drink and additional powdered sport drink mix.

▲ Take iodine tablets (or a filter) to purify the additional water you will need on the trail.

▲ Eat small portions of food and eat often.

▲ Take 200 mg of ibuprofen with lunch and another 200-mg pill in the late afternoon when the aches and pains of the day start to accumulate (take with food).

▲ As the long day wears on, your legs and feet will become extremely tired. Stop and lay down next to a tree or large boulder. Get comfortable. Relax, revitalize, and rejuvenate your legs and feet by elevating them for 5 minutes or more, propping them on a nearby rock or tree. The higher your legs are elevated above your heart, the better. You may look peculiar with your feet pointing skyward, but this will refresh your legs and feet. Rise slowly; sudden movement can cause temporary dizziness and loss of balance.

▲ In your diet, include a balance of carbohydrates and protein at a ratio of about 9 grams of carbohydrates to 7 grams of protein. This has been shown to improve athletes' performance (see discussion of food in Chapter 3).

MOONLIGHT ASCENT

A moonlight ascent is a rewarding way to ascend the peak via the Mount Whitney Trail (Route 6). Because this is a single-day hike, it should be attempted only by those in excellent physical condition because it takes considerable stamina. Arriving on the summit to view the awakening of a new day and the magnificent golden hues of the sunrise is extremely gratifying.

Select a cloudless night with a full moon and wait a couple of hours after moonrise before starting your hike. This will provide a moon-illuminated trail on the eastern slopes at the start of the hike. Later on, the moonlight will touch the western slopes in time to light your crossing from the east to the west side of the divide at Trail Crest.

The nights can be cold, especially if a brisk wind is blowing. Plan for freezing temperatures above 11,000 feet. The coldest time of the night is just before sunrise. If you are on schedule, you will be on or near the summit, the coldest place on the mountain, at the coldest time of the night. Take gloves, a wind parka, wind pants, and a fleece jacket with hood. Carry a flashlight or headlamp and bring extra batteries. You may not need the light, but a few thin clouds could easily obstruct the moonlight. Take ample food and water and follow the applicable recommendations listed under "Trail Tips for a Single-Day Ascent."

If you start your hike before midnight you will need a permit for 2 days; if you depart after midnight, a single-day permit is all you need.

Good luck on your hike to the highest point in the Lower 48! Following any of the thirteen trails and hiking routes described in Chapters 5 and 6 will be a rewarding and enjoyable experience for young and old alike.

Chapter 5

Eastside Trailheads

If you have not visited the east side of the Sierra Nevada, the drive along US 395 will be a wonderful discovery because the area is replete with natural wonders and awesome vistas. From Lake Tahoe in the north to Mount Whitney in the south, the rugged east face escarpment of the Sierra Nevada gradually increases in height and grandeur, culminating atop Mount Whitney, where the spectacular summit rises nearly 10,000 feet above the surrounding terrain. In addition to Lake Tahoe and Mount Whitney, the east side of the Sierra Nevada includes many outstanding geographic features: Twin Lakes, Sawtooth Peaks, Mono Lake, Mono Craters, the Minarets, Devils Postpile National Monument, Little Lakes Valley, Mount Humphrey, Bishop Pass, the Palisades, Kearsarge Pass, University Peak, and Mount Williamson.

Generally, the hiking routes originating on the east side of the Sierra Nevada are shorter and start higher than their counterparts originating on the west side. Because of the topography of the Sierra Nevada, the east side is steep, with short approaches in a dry climate created by the rain and snow shadow of the Sierra Nevada. This is in stark contrast to the west side of the range, where the terrain is more gentle, the approaches are long, and the heavily timbered mountains receive ample rain and snow each year.

The John Muir Trail begins in Yosemite Valley and culminates on the summit of Whitney nearly 225 miles south of its starting point. The John Muir Trail traverses more than 7000 square miles of Sierra Nevada high mountain grandeur. Both eastside and westside trails in this guidebook join the John Muir Trail at various points, some closer to Whitney than others. At one extreme, the Kearsarge Pass Trail (Route 1) joins the John Muir Trail about 30 miles to the north. At the other extreme, the Mount Whitney Trail (Route 6) meets the John Muir Trail only 2 miles south of the summit.

Kearsarge Lakes and Kearsarge Pinnacles (Route 1)

Various eastside routes in this guidebook share common trail segments. For instance, Routes 1, 2, and 3 have different starting points, but they all merge with the John Muir Trail for the ascent. Route 1 (Kearsarge Pass Trail), Route 2 (University Pass Route), and Route 3 (Shepherd Pass Trail) join the John Muir Trail 30, 27, and 17 trail miles north of Whitney.

Route 4 (Circumnavigation Route of Mount Whitney) and Route 5 (Mountaineers Route) start at Whitney Portal and share a common approach for the first 4 miles. Route 4 crosses the Whitney–Russell Col, joining the John Muir Trail at Guitar Lake, whereas Route 5 ascends directly to Whitney's summit via a steep couloir above Iceberg Lake. Route 6 (Mount Whitney Trail) is the main eastside trail to the top of Whitney and the most popular trail in the Sierra Nevada. Route 7 (Meysan Lake Route) and Route 8 (New Army Pass Route) start at different trailheads but share a common cross-country route past beautiful Sky-Blue Lake and Rock Creek. Route 9 (Cottonwood Pass Trail) approaches from the south and joins the John Muir Trail (and Routes 1, 2, and 3) at Crabtree Meadow Patrol Cabin about 8 trail miles from the summit.

All routes in the guidebook can be completed by descending the Mount Whitney Trail (Route 6) for a finish at Whitney Portal. Consequently, hikers starting at trailheads other than Whitney Portal (Routes 1, 2, 3, 8, and 9) need a shuttle (see Appendix 5 for phone numbers of trailhead shuttle services).

HOW TO GET THERE

Road access to the nine eastside trails is via four major east–west arterioles from the towns of Independence and Lone Pine. Independence and Lone Pine are located on US 395, 45 miles and 60 miles south of Bishop, respectively. Lone Pine is about 260 miles south of Reno, Nevada, and about 210 miles north of Los Angeles. Independence is the departure point from US 395 for Onion Valley (Routes 1 and 2) and Shepherd Pass Trailhead (Route 3). Fifteen miles to the south, Lone Pine is the departure point for Whitney Portal (Routes 4–7) and Horseshoe Meadows (Routes 8 and 9). The following table summarizes these east–west access roads to the various eastside trailheads.

Eastside Trailheads

Route	Trailhead and Elevation	Access Road	Nearest Town on US 395	Town to Trailhead
1. Kearsarge Pass Trail	Onion Valley, 9,200 feet	Onion Valley Road	Independence	13.5 miles
2. University Pass Route	Onion Valley, 9,200 feet	Onion Valley Road	Independence	13.5 miles
3. Shepherd Pass Trail	Shepherd Pass Trailhead, 6,240 feet	Onion Valley Road to Foothill Road*	Independence	9.0 miles
4. Circumnavigation of Mount Whitney	Whitney Portal, 8,365 feet	Whitney Portal Road	Lone Pine	13.0 miles
5. Mountaineers Route	Whitney Portal, 8,365 feet	Whitney Portal Road	Lone Pine	13.0 miles
6. Mount Whitney Trail	Whitney Portal, 8,365 feet	Whitney Portal Road	Lone Pine	13.0 miles
7. Meysan Lake Route	Whitney Portal Campground, 8,000 feet	Whitney Portal Road	Lone Pine	12.0 miles
8. New Army Pass Route	Horseshoe Meadow, 10,040 feet	Whitney Portal Rd to Horseshoe Meadow Rd	Lone Pine	24.5 miles
9. Cottonwood Pass Trail	Horseshoe Meadow, 9,920 feet	Same as Route 8 above	Lone Pine	24.0 miles

*All access roads are paved except Foothill Road to Shepherd Pass Trail. It is passable in a sedan.

Route 1: KEARSARGE PASS TRAIL

Trailhead ▲ Onion Valley, 9200 feet

Rating ▲ Class 1

Distance ▲ 39.2 miles to the summit

Elevation gain ▲ 10,771 feet

Effort factor ▲ 30.4 hours

Trip duration ▲ 5–7 days

Maps ▲ Kearsarge Peak, Mount Clarence King, Mount Brewer, Mount Williamson, and Mount Whitney (1:24,000); Mount Pinchot and Mount Whitney (1:62,500); or Tom Harrison Maps, Mount Whitney High Country Trail Map (1:63,360)

Trail Profile Table: Kearsarge Pass Trail

Milepost	Elevation (feet)	Elevation/ Mileage Change	Trail Grade (feet/miles)
Onion Valley (0.0)	9,200	0.0/0.0	0.0
Kearsarge Pass (5.5)	11,760	2,560/5.5	465
Vidette Meadows (9.4)	9,600	-2,200/3.9	-564
Forester Pass (17.4)	13,120	3,520/8.0	440
Shepherd Pass Trail (22.4)	11,000	-2,120/5.0	-424
Crabtree Patrol Cabin (31.2)	10,700	900/8.8	up/down
Guitar Lake (33.7)	11,500	800/2.5	320
Mount Whitney Trail (37.2)	13,480	1,980/3.5	566
Mount Whitney (39.2)	14,491	1,011/2.0	506

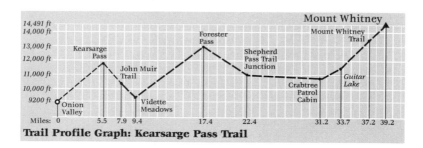

Trail Profile Graph: Kearsarge Pass Trail

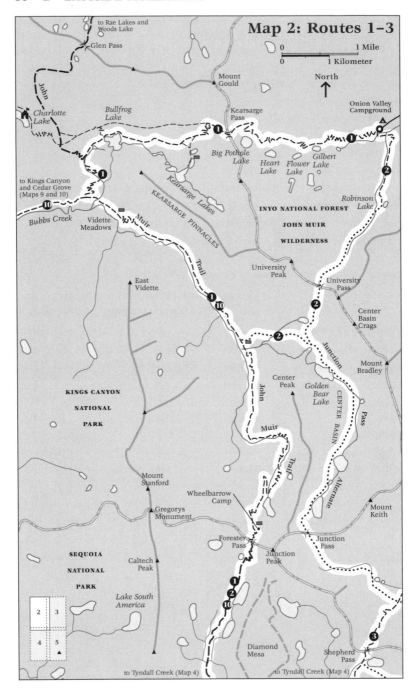

Map 2: Routes 1–3

0   1 Mile
0   1 Kilometer

North

to Rae Lakes and
Woods Lake

Glen Pass

John

Charlotte
Lake

Bullfrog
Lake

Mount
Gould

Kearsarge
Pass

Onion Valley
Campground

Big Pothole
Lake

Heart
Lake

Flower
Lake

Gilbert
Lake

to Kings Canyon
and Cedar Grove
(Maps 9 and 10)

Kearsarge Lakes

KEARSARGE PINNACLES

Robinson
Lake

INYO NATIONAL FOREST

JOHN MUIR

WILDERNESS

Bubbs Creek

Vidette
Meadows

Muir

Trail

East
Vidette

University
Peak

University
Pass

Center
Basin
Crags

KINGS CANYON

NATIONAL

PARK

John

Center
Peak

Golden
Bear
Lake

Junction

CENTER BASIN

Mount
Bradley

Pass

Muir

Mount
Stanford

Gregorys
Monument

Wheelbarrow
Camp

Trail

Alternate

Mount
Keith

SEQUOIA

NATIONAL

PARK

Caltech
Peak

Lake South
America

Forester
Pass

Junction
Peak

Junction
Pass

Shepherd
Pass

2	3
4	5

Diamond
Mesa

to Tyndall Creek (Map 4)

to Tyndall Creek (Map 4)

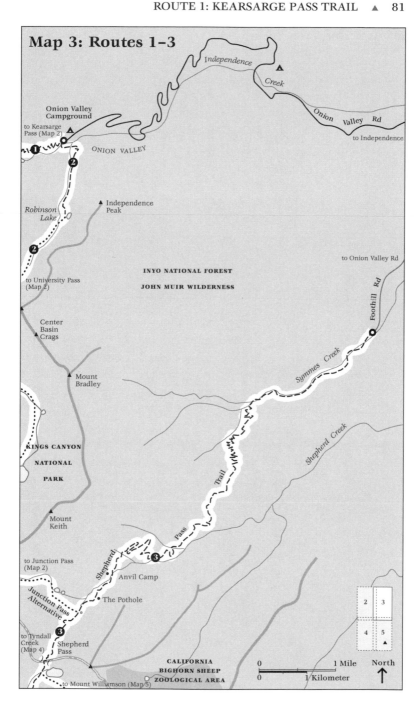

Map 3: Routes 1–3

Independence Creek

Onion Valley Campground

to Kearsarge Pass (Map 2)

ONION VALLEY

Onion Valley Rd

to Independence

Robinson Lake

▲ Independence Peak

to Onion Valley Rd

INYO NATIONAL FOREST

JOHN MUIR WILDERNESS

to University Pass (Map 2)

Foothill Rd

Symmes Creek

Center Basin Crags

▲ Mount Bradley

Shepherd Creek

KINGS CANYON

NATIONAL

PARK

Pass Trail

▲ Mount Keith

Shepherd

to Junction Pass (Map 2)

Anvil Camp

Junction Pass Alternative

The Pothole

to Tyndall Creek (Map 4)

Shepherd Pass

CALIFORNIA
BIGHORN SHEEP
ZOOLOGICAL AREA

to Mount Williamson (Map 5)

| 2 | 3 |
| 4 | 5 |

0   1 Mile
0   1/Kilometer

North

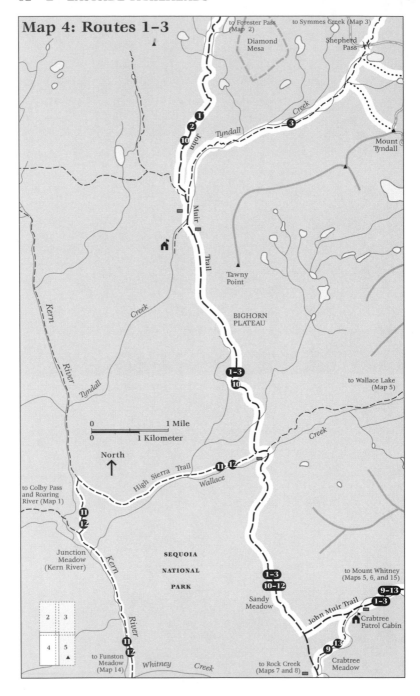

Map 4: Routes 1–3

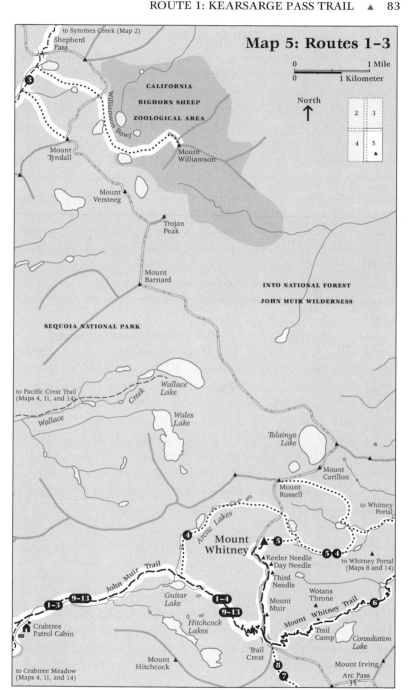

Map 5: Routes 1–3

to Symmes Creek (Map 2)
Shepherd Pass

❸

CALIFORNIA

BIGHORN SHEEP

ZOOLOGICAL AREA

Williamson Bowl

Mount Tyndall

Mount Williamson

Mount Versteeg

Trojan Peak

Mount Barnard

INYO NATIONAL FOREST

JOHN MUIR WILDERNESS

SEQUOIA NATIONAL PARK

to Pacific Crest Trail
(Maps 4, 11, and 14)

Wallace Creek

Wallace Lake

Wales Lake

Wallace

Tulainyo Lake

Mount Carillon

Mount Russell

to Whitney Portal

❹ Arctic Lakes

Mount Whitney

❺

Keeler Needle
Day Needle

❺❹

to Whitney Portal
(Maps 8 and 14)

John Muir Trail

Guitar Lake

❶-❹

Third Needle

Wotans Throne

Mount Muir

Mount Whitney Trail

❻

❶-❸ ❾-❶❸

❾-❶❸

Hitchcock Lakes

Crabtree Patrol Cabin

Trail Camp

Consultation Lake

Mount Hitchcock

Trail Crest

❽

❼

Mount Irving

to Crabtree Meadow
(Maps 4, 11, and 14)

Arc Pass

0 ——————— 1 Mile
0 ——————— 1 Kilometer

North
↑

| 2 | 3 |
| 4 | 5 ▲ |

IN A NUTSHELL

Once an Indian trading route, Kearsarge Pass Trail now provides direct access to beautiful Kearsarge Lakes basin, the spectacular backcountry of the John Muir Wilderness, and Sequoia and Kings Canyon National Parks. From the 9200-foot trailhead at Onion Valley, the trail ascends nearly 2600 feet to Kearsarge Pass and then quickly descends 2200 feet past Kearsarge Lakes and Bullfrog Lake to the rich Vidette Meadows, Bubbs Creek, and the John Muir Trail. The route then follows Bubbs Creek and the John Muir Trail as it ascends a beautiful glaciated valley, gaining 3500 feet to the highest pass on the John Muir Trail (Forester Pass), where the trail crosses the Kings–Kern Divide. From the pass the trail drops 2100 feet to Tyndall Creek and then passes by Wallace Creek, Crabtree Meadow, and Guitar Lake. From Guitar Lake the trail climbs nearly 3000 feet on its way to the summit of Whitney. This is a popular route, so make your reservation early.

The shortest trans-Sierra hike from road end to road end is Onion Valley to Roads End in Kings Canyon National Park. Each year for the past 20 years a small group of faithful hikers from southern California have competed in what they call the Trans-Sierra Classic and celebrated with a large meal at a campground near Cedar Grove. This hike starts at Onion Valley, ascends Kearsarge Pass, descends to Vidette Meadows, and descends the Bubbs Creek Trail, passing through Junction Meadow (Bubbs Creek), and continuing to Roads End. The Trans-Sierra Classic uses portions of both Route 1 (Kearsarge Pass Trail) and Route 10 (Bubbs Creek Trail).

TRAILHEAD FACILITIES

Potable water is available at the trailhead. A 29-unit campground is located nearby. Metal bear-proof food lockers are located at the campsites. The campground usually is open May through September. The 52-unit Lower and Upper Greys Meadow Campground is located 6 miles west of Independence on the Onion Valley Road and usually is open March through October.

HOW TO GET THERE

From the town of Independence on US 395 (45 miles south of Bishop), turn west on Market Street (Onion Valley Road) and drive 13.5 miles to Onion Valley, located at the end of the road. The paved road usually is open from May to November.

BEAR-PROOF WILDERNESS FOOD STORAGE BOX LOCATIONS

▲ **Kearsarge Lakes:** One box is located on the Kearsarge Lakes lateral trail at the south end of the upper small lakes, a second box on the north shore of the largest upper lake, and a third box on the north shore of the lowest small lake.

▲ **Vidette Meadows:** One box is located at Lower Vidette Meadow about 0.1 mile west of the John Muir Trail junction on the south side of the Bubbs Creek Trail; the second box at East Vidette is located about 0.2 mile on the John Muir Trail above the Bubbs Creek–John Muir Trail junction on the south side of the trail.

▲ **John Muir Trail and Center Basin Trail:** One box has been placed below the trail approximately 150 yards south of the trail junction (0.25 mile north of the Center Basin Creek crossing).

▲ **Wheelbarrow Camp:** One box is located in the first group of trees north of Forester Pass.

▲ **John Muir Trail and Tyndall Creek Crossing:** One box is located west of the trail, about 350 feet north of the creek.

▲ **Tyndall Creek Frog Ponds:** One box is located about 0.5 mile south of Tyndall Creek Crossing on the east side of the trail.

▲ **John Muir Trail and Wallace Creek Crossing:** One box is located west of the trail about 100 feet south of the creek crossing.

▲ **Crabtree Meadow:** One box is located southeast of the creek and about 0.1 mile south of the Crabtree Patrol Cabin near the creek crossing.

ROUTE DESCRIPTION

Mile 0 to 5.5 (Onion Valley to Kearsarge Pass)
The trail gains elevation steadily as it climbs from Onion Valley to Kearsarge Pass, an elevation gain of 2560 feet over 5.5 miles. The trail

begins by ascending a series of switchbacks passing Little Pothole Lake, Gilbert Lake, and Flower Lake. In the first couple of miles, deer often are seen early in the morning or near dusk. The trail ascends high above Heart Lake by way of more switchbacks, providing great views of this heart-shaped lake. Above Heart Lake, a large glacial moraine acts as a natural dam holding back the waters of Big Pothole Lake. The trail passes Big Pothole Lake, making its final climb to Kearsarge Pass. On the hike to Kearsarge Pass you are rewarded with impressive views (to your left) of University Peak (13,632 feet). At Kearsarge Pass the trail passes from the John Muir Wilderness to Kings Canyon National Park. From the pass there are expansive views into Kings Canyon National Park, including Kearsarge Pinnacles, Kearsarge Lakes, Bullfrog Lake, Mount Brewer, and North Guard.

Mile 5.5 to 9.4 (Kearsarge Pass to Vidette Meadows)

From Kearsarge Pass it is about 2.4 miles to the junction of the John Muir Trail and another 1.5 miles south along the John Muir Trail to Vidette Meadows. The trail drops 2200 feet over this 3.9-mile segment, passing Kearsarge Lakes and Bullfrog Lake before joining the John Muir Trail near Vidette Meadows. Immediately west of Kearsarge Pass (about 5 minutes of hiking) the trail forks; take the left fork leading to Kearsarge Lakes (0.6 mile) and Bullfrog Lake. Bullfrog Lake is closed to camping, but there are three bear-proof food storage lockers at Kearsarge Lakes, with a one-night limit on camping because of the heavy use in the area. Camp at Kearsarge Lakes or continue down to Vidette Meadows.

Vidette Meadows are notorious for bear activity. However, if you use the food storage lockers placed by the National Park Service, you should have no problems with bears. As you descend the trail into the deep canyon containing Bubbs Creek, Vidette Meadows, and the John Muir Trail, there are many fine vistas of East Vidette. East Vidette is not the highest peak in the area but is one of the most striking.

Mile 9.4 to 17.4 (Vidette Meadows to Forester Pass)

The hike up the north side of the Kings–Kern Divide to Forester Pass is a wonderful climb. Lush meadows, small lakes, beautiful wildflowers, and cascading streams are surrounded by the towering summits of Mount Stanford, Junction Peak, and Basin Peak. The trail gains elevation at a gradual but steady rate of 500 feet per mile.

Forester Pass is the highest pass on the John Muir Trail as it crests the Kings–Kern Divide at 13,120 feet. Here the trail passes from Kings Canyon National Park to Sequoia National Park. From Vidette Meadows it is about 3.5 miles to the Center Basin Trail junction and another 4.5 miles of steady climbing to Forester Pass. Center Basin Trail junction is the point where Route 2 joins Route 1 and the John Muir Trail. There is a bear-proof food storage box at this trail junction and another at Wheelbarrow Camp, north of Forester Pass in a group of trees.

Junction Pass Alternative

Consider this alternative route in heavy snow years because it bypasses Forester Pass and the steep snow-filled gullies on the south side of the pass. Junction Pass is the original route of the John Muir Trail and was used until 1932, when the trail over Forester Pass was built. The trail has not been maintained for nearly 70 years, but portions of the trail can still be seen. About 3.5 miles south of Vidette Meadows, take the Center Basin Trail and ascend to Golden Bear Lake, passing the lake on its north and east sides. Follow the Center Basin Trail for about 0.5 mile beyond Golden Bear Lake. Here the trail fades into the talus. Continue to the upper two lakes in Center Basin, passing to the west and ascending scree slopes to Junction Pass. Junction Pass is 13,200 feet and about 0.4 mile northeast of Junction Peak. On the south side of the pass, descend sand and scree to the valley between Junction Peak and Junction Pass. Stay on the north side of the valley. After a short distance, cross to the west side of the stream and descend to a bench and meadow before reaching the Shepherd Pass Trail near the Pothole. Ascend the Shepherd Pass Trail to Shepherd Pass and hike down the west side over gentle terrain to the John Muir Trail.

Mile 17.4 to 22.4 (Forester Pass to Shepherd Pass Trail)

The south side of Forester Pass is steep, with the trail switchbacking down and through large granite cliffs. Near the top of the pass the trail crosses several steep gullies. These gullies may be filled with snow in June and July. You may need crampons to cross these narrow, steep chutes. Check with the Sequoia National Park Ranger Station for trail conditions (see Appendix 5). Continue down to the junction of the Shepherd Pass Trail. There are two bear-proof food storage boxes near the junction of the Shepherd Pass trail: one where the John Muir Trail crosses Tyndall Creek and the other 0.5 mile south of the Tyndall Creek crossing near the frog ponds.

If you plan a side trip to climb Mount Tyndall (14,019 feet) or Mount Williamson (14,370 feet), hike up the Shepherd Pass Trail to near the pass, a 4-mile hike through meadows and along streams over gradual terrain. The route descriptions to climb Mount Tyndall and Mount Williamson are included in the Shepherd Pass Trail (Route 3).

Mile 22.4 to 31.2
(Shepherd Pass Trail to Crabtree Patrol Cabin)

The trail continues past Tawny Point and crosses the Bighorn Plateau. Over this 4.6-mile section of trail there is a net loss of 500 feet in elevation, but the trail includes some short climbs over gentle terrain. The views from Bighorn Plateau of the Kern Canyon, the Great Western Divide, and the Kaweahs are expansive. There is a bear-proof food storage box near the Wallace Creek trail crossing.

From Wallace Creek, the trail climbs about 500 feet in the first mile then drops 300 feet toward Sandy Meadow. The trail again begins to climb, gaining 200 feet, and then drops slightly to a trail junction 3.3 miles from Wallace Creek. At this trail junction, the Pacific Crest Trail continues south, and the John Muir Trail turns east (left) toward Mount Whitney. Turn left and hike 0.9 mile to the Crabtree Meadow. There is a bear-proof food storage box near the creek crossing about 0.1 mile before the Crabtree Patrol Cabin.

Mile 31.2 to 33.7 (Crabtree Patrol Cabin to Guitar Lake)

Over the next 2.5 miles the trail ascends gradually to Guitar Lake. After about 0.25 mile a pond is passed, and after another mile and a short climb the trail passes Timberline Lake. From this lake, sandwiched between granite cliffs and timber, the trail gains 500 feet to Guitar Lake. If you are looking for a campsite, consider Guitar Lake and its many fine sites or hike past the lake for about 0.3 mile and camp near a tarn at the 11,600-foot level. Alternatively, continue to the 11,900-foot level, where there are numerous fine campsites near a series of tarns linked by a small stream flowing toward Hitchcock Lakes. These campsites have rewarding views of Guitar Lake below and the granite slopes of Mount Whitney above.

Mile 33.7 to 37.2 (Guitar Lake to Mount Whitney Trail)

From Guitar Lake, the John Muir Trail climbs steadily for 3.5 miles and nearly 2000 feet up the steep west slopes of Mount Whitney. A series of switchbacks seems endless but finally ends at the junction with the Mount Whitney Trail. The views of Hitchcock Lakes, Guitar Lake, and the mountain panorama improve as you gain elevation. The trail itself is impressive as it climbs through talus, large rock faces, and impressive granite towers. This segment of trail and the ninety-seven switchbacks below Trail Crest on the east side (Mount Whitney Trail, Route 6) are engineering marvels and tributes to the workers who built them. There are several large tent platforms at the John Muir–Mount Whitney Trail junction that can serve as campsites, but you must bring water because these are dry campsites.

Mile 37.2 to 39.2
(Mount Whitney Trail to Mount Whitney)

There are only 2 more miles to the summit and a little more than 1000 feet of elevation gain. The most difficult hiking is over as the John Muir Trail gradually reaches the highest point in the Lower 48. Drop your pack and head for the summit. If you are not suffering from the altitude, the next 2 miles will be enjoyable as the trail snakes its way through impressive rock towers and past windows in the Sierra Nevada crest that provide breathtaking views of Trail Camp, the Mount Whitney Trail, and the Owens Valley far below. On the other hand, this may be the most strenuous portion of the trip because the altitude may have depleted your energy, strength, and desire to continue.

The trail along the west side of the crest provides an excellent opportunity to scramble up Mount Muir and to bag the four 14,000-foot subpeaks of Mount Whitney: Aiguille Extra, Third Needle, Crooks Peak (also known as Day Needle), and Keeler Needle. Each of these peaks is only a couple of hundred feet above the trail. From the junction of the Mount Whitney Trail, ascend the two switchbacks and proceed to a large rock cairn marking the cutoff to Mount Muir. The summit of Muir is visible from this point on the trail. Ascend a shallow gully of loose scree and head toward the notch in the ridge to the right of the main summit. From this notch, angle left and climb a small chimney. Traverse left across a sloping ledge. Climb a crack to your right, gaining the small summit block. There is room for only three or four carefully placed climbers on the top at any one time. The top 50 feet of climbing is easy Class 3. From the summit there are impressive views of the east face of Mount Muir directly below, ninety-seven switchbacks in the Mount Whitney Trail, Trail Camp,

Consultation Lake, Arc Pass, Whitney Portal, and the Owens Valley far below.

To ascend any of the four 14,000-foot subpeaks of Whitney, leave the John Muir Trail and scramble up the west slopes to the summit of these needles. All are easy Class 2 scrambles and provide a bird's-eye view of the sheer, near-vertical east face. The top of each needle is visible from the trail. To climb the first needle, Aiguille Extra, leave the John Muir Trail about 1 mile from the junction of the Mount Whitney Trail and scramble to the top. The others follow in quick succession. For the last and highest needle, Keeler Needle, leave the John Muir Trail just before it turns west heading away from the crest to begin the final climb to the summit of Whitney.

On the summit of Whitney you will be greeted with impressive views of Mount Langley and Mount Muir to the south; the Kaweah Mountains and Sawtooth Peak to the west; Mount Russell, Tulainyo Lake (to the right of Mount Russell), the highest large alpine lake in the Sierra Nevada, Mount Williamson, Milestone Mountain, Table Mountain, and Thunder Mountain to the north; and Trail Camp, Mount Whitney Trail switchbacks, Consultation Lake, and Owens Valley to the east. If the weather is pleasant, spend some time on top; take in the scenery. This is an accomplishment you will long remember.

Return to your pack and hike out the Mount Whitney Trail. For a description of the trail, refer to Route 6.

Route 2: UNIVERSITY PASS ROUTE

Trailhead ▲ Onion Valley, 9200 feet
Rating ▲ Class 2
Distance ▲ 32.1 miles to the summit
Elevation gain ▲ 10,711 feet
Effort factor ▲ 26.8 hours
Trip duration ▲ 5–7 days
Maps ▲ Kearsarge Peak, Mount Brewer, Mount Williamson, and Mount Whitney (1:24,000); Mount Pinchot and Mount Whitney (1:62,500); or Tom Harrison Maps, Mount Whitney High Country (1:63,360)

Trail Profile Table: University Pass Route

Milepost	Elevation (feet)	Elevation/ Mileage Change	Trail Grade (feet/miles)
Onion Valley (0.0)	9,200	0.0/0.0	0.0
Robinson Lake (2.0)	10,500	1,300/2.0	650
University Pass (3.8)	12,600	2,100/1.8	1,400
John Muir Trail (5.3)	10,500	-2,100/1.5	-1,400
Forester Pass (10.3)	13,120	2,620/5.0	524
Shepherd Pass Trail (15.3)	11,000	-2,120/5.0	-424
Crabtree Patrol Cabin (24.1)	10,700	900/8.8	up/down
Guitar Lake (26.6)	11,500	800/2.5	320
Mount Whitney Trail (30.1)	13,480	1,980/3.5	566
Mount Whitney (32.1)	14,491	1,011/2.0	506

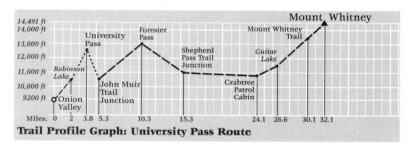

Trail Profile Graph: University Pass Route

IN A NUTSHELL

This route starts at Onion Valley and bypasses Kearsarge Pass and the deep recess of Vidette Meadows. Start by following the Robinson Lake Trail to Robinson Lake, and then continue cross-country over University Pass. From University Pass descend loose scree to Center Basin and the John Muir Trail. This route is about 7 miles shorter than the Kearsarge Pass Trail (Route 1), which also starts at Onion Valley, but contains rugged cross-country travel over University Pass.

The Robinson Lake Trail ends at the lake, leaving one to ascend University Pass via a cross-country route (Class 2) over large boulders and scree. The cross-country route is short (3.3 miles) but strenuous.

Take crampons and ice ax for the short scramble up University Pass. There is usually snow in the couloir through August.

The cross-country travel is over rugged terrain that is not technically difficult but is strenuous. Hikers with a moderate degree of route-finding experience using a map and compass should not have difficulty following this route. A wilderness permit for the Robinson Lake Trail can be easily secured because the quota for the trail is seldom reached. Ask to enter the Mount Whitney Zone when securing your wilderness permit.

TRAILHEAD FACILITIES

Potable water is available at Onion Valley. The 29-unit Onion Valley Campground is located near the trailhead. Metal bear-proof food lockers are located at the campsites. The campground usually is open May through September. The 52-unit Lower and Upper Greys Meadow Campground is located 6 miles west of Independence on Onion Valley Road and usually is open March through October.

HOW TO GET THERE

From the town of Independence on US 395 (45 miles south of Bishop), turn west on Market Street (Onion Valley Road) and drive 13.5 miles to Onion Valley, located at the end of the road. The paved road usually is open from May to November.

BEAR-PROOF WILDERNESS FOOD STORAGE BOX LOCATIONS

- ▲ **John Muir Trail and Center Basin Trail:** One box is located below the trail approximately 150 yards south of the trail junction (0.25 mile north of the Center Basin Creek crossing).
- ▲ **Wheelbarrow Camp:** One box is located in the first group of trees north of Forester Pass.
- ▲ **John Muir Trail and Tyndall Creek Crossing:** One box is located west of the trail about 350 feet north of the creek.
- ▲ **Tyndall Creek Frog Ponds:** One box is located about 0.5 mile south of Tyndall Creek Crossing on the east side of the trail.
- ▲ **John Muir Trail and Wallace Creek Crossing:** One box is located west of the trail about 100 feet south of the creek crossing.

▲ **Crabtree Meadow:** One box is located southeast of the creek and about 0.1 mile south of the Crabtree Patrol Cabin near the creek crossing.

ROUTE DESCRIPTION

Mile 0 to 2 (Onion Valley to Robinson Lake)

The start of the trail is not well signed and begins in the Onion Valley Campground, next to campsite 8. The Robinson Lake Trail has not been maintained for many years, and there is some brush, but the trail is easy to follow because numerous rock cairns mark the way. From the eastern end of the Onion Valley Campground, the trail heads south to Robinson Lake and a large hanging valley. The trail climbs steeply to the lake, gaining 1300 feet in about 2 miles. This short, steep trail passes through large stands of virgin timber and groves of Aspen trees. Deer are common in the area and may be seen early in the morning. The trail ascends the glacial moraine far to the left of the lake's outlet stream. At the top of the moraine, many trees have been uprooted by powerful avalanches that have swept down the steep slopes of Independence Peak.

Mile 2 to 3.8 (Robinson Lake to University Pass)

The trail ends at Robinson Lake, signaling the start of the cross-country route from Robinson Lake to University Pass. The route is over rough terrain but is easy to follow as it parallels the Robinson Lake inlet stream. An occasional rock cairn marks this popular climber's route to University Pass and University Peak. Hike around the right side of Robinson Lake, passing through a large stand of timber. Ascend a minor rib to the right of the inlet creek and follow it to about 11,600 feet. At this point, traverse into the creek drainage. Two prominent passes are now visible. Both passes lead to Center Basin and the John Muir Trail. University Pass is the lowest point between University Peak and Peak 3926 meters (12,910 feet) and is about 0.6 mile southeast of University Peak. Depending on the amount of snowfall the previous winter, snow usually remains in the couloir below University Pass into August, necessitating crampons and ice ax. Ascend either gully to the pass. The route from Robinson Lake to University Pass gains 2100 feet in only 1.8 miles. The route is not particularly steep for most of the distance but significantly steepens in the couloir below the pass. At University Pass the route enters Sequoia National Park.

University Pass is on the right. Both the passes pictured lead to Center Basin and the John Muir Trail (Route 2).

Mile 3.8 to 5.3 (University Pass to the John Muir Trail)
Descend the west side of the pass by way of a long chute filled with loose scree. Pass by the unnamed lake at 11,200 feet and continue on to the Center Basin trail. Follow this trail west to the John Muir Trail. At the junction with the John Muir Trail, turn south (left) and begin the magnificent climb up the canyon to Forester Pass. There is a bear-proof food storage locker at the junction of the Center Basin and John Muir Trails.

Mile 5.3 to 10.3 (John Muir Trail to Forester Pass)
Refer to Route 1 for the details of this trail segment and for the Junction Pass alternative to Forester Pass. Consider the Junction Pass alternative in heavy snow years to avoid the steep snow gullies on the south side of Forester Pass.

Mile 10.3 to 15.3 (Forester Pass to Shepherd Pass Trail)

Refer to Route 1 for the details of this trail segment. If you plan a side trip to Mount Tyndall (14,019 feet) or Mount Williamson (14,370 feet), hike up the Shepherd Pass Trail to near the pass, a 4-mile hike through meadows and along streams over gradual terrain. The route descriptions for climbing Mount Tyndall and Mount Williamson are included in the Shepherd Pass Trail description (Route 3).

Mile 15.3 to 24.1
(Shepherd Pass Trail to Crabtree Patrol Cabin)

Refer to Route 1 for the details of this trail segment.

Mile 24.1 to 26.6 (Crabtree Patrol Cabin to Guitar Lake)

Refer to Route 1 for the details of this trail segment.

Mile 26.6 to 30.1 (Guitar Lake to Mount Whitney Trail)

Refer to Route 1 for the details of this trail segment.

Mile 30.1 to 32.1
(Mount Whitney Trail to Mount Whitney Summit)

Refer to Route 1 for the details of this trail segment. After summiting, return to your pack at the junction of the John Muir Trail and the Mount Whitney Trail and hike out the Mount Whitney Trail. For a trail description, refer to Route 6.

Route 3: SHEPHERD PASS TRAIL

Trailhead ▲ Symmes Creek, 6240 feet

Rating ▲ Class 1

Distance ▲ 29 miles to the summit

Elevation gain ▲ 10,951 feet

Effort factor ▲ 25.5 hours

Trip duration ▲ 4–6 days

Maps ▲ Mount Williamson, Mount Brewer, and Mount Whitney (1:24,000); Mount Pinchot and Mount Whitney (1:62,500); or Tom Harrison Maps, Mount Whitney High Country (1:63,360)

Trail Profile Table: Shepherd Pass Trail

Milepost	Elevation (feet)	Elevation/ Mileage Change	Trail Grade (feet/miles)
Symmes Creek (0.0)	6,240	0.0/0.0	0.0
Trail divide (3.0)	9,200	2,960/3.0	987
Shepherd Canyon (4.0)	8,700	-500/1.0	-500
Shepherd Pass (8.0)	12,000	3,300/4.0	825
John Muir Trail (12.2)	11,000	-1,000/4.2	-238
Crabtree Patrol Cabin (21.0)	10,700	900/8.8	up/down
Guitar Lake (23.5)	11,500	800/2.5	320
Mount Whitney Trail (27.0)	13,480	1,980/3.5	566
Mount Whitney (29.0)	14,491	1,011/2.0	506

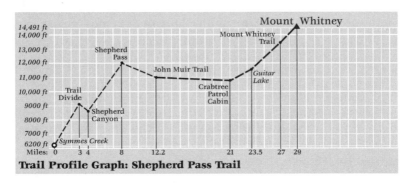

Trail Profile Graph: Shepherd Pass Trail

IN A NUTSHELL

The Shepherd Pass Trail is long and arduous, with numerous steep portions. The trail gains more than 6000 feet before reaching Shepherd Pass after 8 tough miles. The trail begins at Symmes Creek and follows the creek for a mile, crossing the stream four times before ascending steeply to the ridge dividing Symmes Creek and Shepherd Creek. At the Symmes–Shepherd Creek divide (located some distance east of the main Sierra Nevada crest) the trail drops 500 feet to Shepherd Creek. From this new low point, the trail gains 3300 feet in 4 miles to Shepherd Pass. From the pass, it is an easy and enjoyable 4.2-mile hike through meadows and along streams to the junction with the John Muir Trail. The Shepherd Pass Trail is strenuous but does not involve cross-country travel. It is a shorter route to Mount Whitney than Route 1 (Kearsarge Pass Trail) and Route 2 (University Pass Route) because it cuts off about 10 miles and 3 miles, respectively.

This route also affords an excellent opportunity to climb Mount Tyndall and Mount Williamson, two 14,000-footers. Mount Williamson is the second highest peak in California at 14,370 feet.

You can obtain a wilderness permit reservation for the Shepherd Pass Trail with little difficulty, especially if you are departing during midweek. Indicate that you plan to enter the Mount Whitney Zone when securing your wilderness permit.

TRAILHEAD FACILITIES

There are no trailhead facilities.

HOW TO GET THERE

From the town of Independence (45 miles south of Bishop) on US 395, turn west on Market Street (Onion Valley Road) and drive 4.3 miles to Foothill Road and turn left (south). Follow this dirt road for 1.3 miles and turn right at the fork. Proceed 1.6 miles to a horse corral. Continue past the corral for 0.4 mile to the next fork. Turn right (west) and drive 0.5 mile to the next fork and turn right. In 0.9 mile you will reach the end of the road and the Shepherd Pass Trail that ascends Symmes Creek. The dirt road to the Shepherd Pass trailhead is passable in a sedan (i.e., a high-clearance vehicle is not needed).

BEAR-PROOF WILDERNESS FOOD STORAGE BOX LOCATIONS

- ▲ **John Muir Trail and Tyndall Creek Crossing:** One box is located west of the trail about 350 feet north of the creek.
- ▲ **Tyndall Creek Frog Ponds:** One box is located about 0.5 mile south of Tyndall Creek Crossing on the east side of the trail.
- ▲ **John Muir Trail and Wallace Creek Crossing:** One box has been placed west of the trail about 100 feet south of the creek crossing.
- ▲ **Crabtree Meadow:** One box is located southeast of the creek and about 0.1 mile south of the Crabtree Patrol Cabin near the creek crossing.

ROUTE DESCRIPTION

Mile 0 to 3 (Symmes Creek to trail divide)

There are two starting points for the Shepherd Pass trail: one for hikers and one for stock. The one for stock starts near a corral at the 5700-foot level and adds 1.25 miles to the approach. The hiker's trail begins at 6240 feet, a low starting elevation for trails on the east side of the Sierra Nevada. Over the first mile (from the hiker's trailhead) the trail follows Symmes Creek, crossing it four times before starting a 2-mile climb up numerous switchbacks to a saddle in the ridge that divides Symmes Creek and Shepherd Creek. The trail is steep but not unpleasant because it is on the north (cool) side of the ridge and is shaded by large stands of virgin evergreen trees. Once you leave Symmes Creek there is no water for about 4 miles, so make sure your water bottles are full.

Mile 3 to 4 (trail divide to Shepherd Canyon)

At the crest of the ridge (9200 feet), the trail crosses a broad saddle where the trail traverses the hot hillside to a notch 0.25 mile away. Here the virgin forest coverage gives way to mountain mahogany and chaparral. Little shade from the hot summer sun can now be found. At this notch, the trail starts its descent (including several switchbacks) into Shepherd Canyon, dropping about 500 feet.

Mile 4 to 8 (Shepherd Canyon to Shepherd Pass)

From this new low point (8700 feet), the trail begins a 2-mile, 1700-foot climb to Anvil Camp. Near Anvil Camp the trail crosses Shepherd Creek for the first time. In another 0.75 mile the trail crosses the creek again near the Pothole (not to be confused with Big Pothole Lake on the Kearsarge Pass Trail, Route 1). Campsites are available at Anvil Camp and the Pothole, but if you can, continue to the large lake at 12,000 feet west of Shepherd Pass. From the Pothole, the trail continues through moraines, talus, boulder fields, and snowfields (in June and July) to Shepherd Pass and Sequoia National Park. East of the crest the trail enters the Bighorn Sheep Zoological Area. Please respect the area closures (as noted on the USGS maps).

From Shepherd Pass, there are two wonderful opportunities to climb Mount Tyndall (14,019 feet) and Mount Williamson (14,370 feet).

Mount Tyndall from near Shepherd Pass

To climb Mount Tyndall, ascend the northwest slope to the summit ridge. These slopes are Class 2 scrambles. Once the summit ridge is gained, it is a short climb to the main summit. Stay on the crest of the summit ridge or drop down slightly to the southwest of the ridge. There are a couple of short sections along the summit ridge where there is some airy exposure.

A climb of Mount Williamson is a more serious endeavor and entails some Class 3 climbing and routefinding skills. Allocate a full day to climb Mount Williamson from Shepherd Pass. At 14,370 feet, Mount Williamson is the second highest peak in the Sierra Nevada, only 121 feet lower than Whitney. The peak has two secondary summits, both higher than 14,000 feet. Mount Williamson is the most massive of all the Sierra Nevada peaks and is an impressive sight from all directions, especially from the east and US 395 near the town of Independence, nearly 2 vertical miles below. The route to the base of the mountain leads through the Williamson Bowl, one of the more inaccessible and unique areas in the Sierra Nevada. A day trip into the Williamson Bowl, even if you do not plan a climb of Mount Williamson, is worth the effort. This area is in the California Bighorn Sheep Zoological Area, and the few remaining bighorn sheep are on the verge of extinction, so please adhere to the closure dates for this area.

From Shepherd Pass, hike southeast past the unnamed lake at 12,000 feet and another small, unnamed lake at 12,400 feet to the saddle leading to the Williamson Bowl. Descend to the bowl on large boulders and talus but stay on the ridge that bisects the bowl. There are lakes on either side of this ridge. Head to the unnamed lake near Mount Versteeg located just below the 12,400-foot level. From this lake, head toward Mount Williamson and the most prominent black stains. These black stains have been formed over the centuries by the continuous running of water over the rocks. Above these large black stains, enter a narrow chute that angles up and to the left. Follow this chute almost all the way to the crest. Near the top, climb right for about 100 feet to a 60-foot, Class 3 chimney. This short pitch leads to the summit plateau and easy hiking to the true summit. The views from the summit are impressive, with Mount Tyndall, Shepherd Pass, the Kings-Kern Divide, and Mount Whitney all nearby.

Mile 8 to 12.2 (Shepherd Pass to junction with the John Muir Trail)

It is an easy and enjoyable walk over gentle terrain down to the John Muir Trail. Meadows, creeks, flowers, and beautiful vistas highlight this trail segment. In 4.2 miles the trail drops only 1000 feet.

Mile 12.2 to 21 (John Muir Trail and Shepherd Pass Trail Junction to Crabtree Patrol Cabin)

Refer to Route 1 for the details of this trail segment.

Mile 21 to 23.5 (Crabtree Patrol Cabin to Guitar Lake)

Refer to Route 1 for the details of this trail segment.

Mile 23.5 to 27 (Guitar Lake to Mount Whitney Trail)

Refer to Route 1 for the details of this trail segment.

Mile 27 to 29 (Mount Whitney Trail to Mount Whitney)

Refer to Route 1 for the details of this trail segment. After summiting, return to your pack at the junction of the John Muir Trail and the Mount Whitney Trail and hike out the Mount Whitney Trail. For a description of this trail, refer to Route 6.

Route 4: CIRCUMNAVIGATION ROUTE OF MOUNT WHITNEY

Trailhead ▲ Whitney Portal, 8365 feet

Rating ▲ Class 2

Distance ▲ 12 miles to the summit

Elevation gain ▲ 7686 feet

Effort factor ▲ 13.7 hours

Trip duration ▲ 4–6 days

Maps ▲ Mount Whitney (1:24,000); Mount Whitney (1:62,500); or Tom Harrison Maps, Mount Whitney High Country (1:63,360)

Trail Profile Table: Circumnavigation Route of Mount Whitney

Milepost	Elevation (feet)	Elevation/ Mileage Change	Trail Grade (feet/miles)
Whitney Portal (0.0)	8,365	0.0/0.0	0.0
North Fork Lone Pine Creek (0.8)	8,700	335/0.8	419
Lower Boy Scout Lake (1.8)	10,300	1,600/1.0	1,600
Upper Boy Scout Lake (2.7)	11,300	1,000/0.9	1,111
Whitney–Russell Col (4.3)	13,060	1,760/1.6	1,100
Guitar Lake (6.5)	11,500	-700/2.2	-875
Mount Whitney Trail (10.0)	13,480	1,980/3.5	566
Mount Whitney (12.0)	14,491	1,011/2.0	506

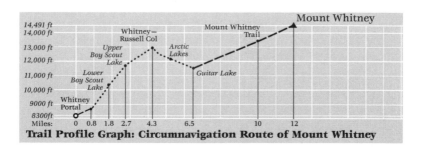

Trail Profile Graph: Circumnavigation Route of Mount Whitney

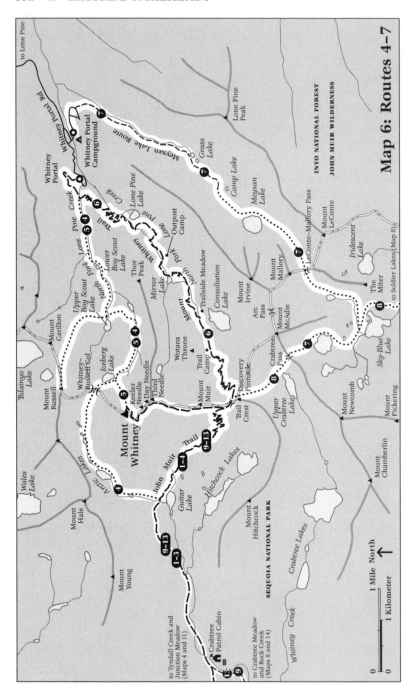

Map 6: Routes 4–7

IN A NUTSHELL

The Circumnavigation Route of Mount Whitney is one of the finest routes featured in this guidebook. This exceptional trip ascends the North Fork Lone Pine Creek, traverses beneath the spectacular east and north faces of Whitney, crosses the Whitney–Russell Col, and passes through the seldom-visited Arctic Lakes recess, joining the John Muir Trail near Guitar Lake, where it follows the trail to the summit. The route also provides an excellent opportunity to climb Mount Russell (14,088 feet, Class 3 +) or Mount Carillon (Class 2).

The route over the Whitney–Russell Col involves some cross-country travel, but routefinding is straightforward. The terrain above Iceberg Lake and down through the Arctic Lakes recess is surprisingly gentle considering that it is sandwiched between the impressive north face of Whitney and the striking Fishhook Arête of Mount Russell.

The route includes 6.3 miles over maintained trails (Class 1), 3.1 miles over an unmaintained climber's route (Class 2), and 2.6 miles cross-country without the benefit of any type of trail (Class 2). The 5.7 miles of cross-country travel traverses rugged terrain that is strenuous but not technically difficult. Hikers with a moderate degree of route-finding experience using a map and compass should be able to follow this fine route. This route, Route 8, and Route 11 are my favorites.

Gene Leach on the Ebersbacher Ledges ascending Route 4

TRAILHEAD FACILITIES

The Whitney Portal Store and Cafe supplies basic meals, souvenirs, tee shirts, sweatshirts, books, maps, bear-proof canisters, showers (bring your own towel), and a cellular pay phone (bring money). There is a ten-unit hiker campground near the trailhead. Near the store there is a picnic area with barbecue grills, tables, and a fishing pond. One mile to the east is a forty-four–unit campground with piped water and vault toilets.

HOW TO GET THERE

From the signal light in the town of Lone Pine on US 395 drive 13 miles west on the Whitney Portal Road to its end. The paved road usually is open from May to early November. In the winter the last 6 miles of the road are not plowed.

BEAR-PROOF WILDERNESS FOOD STORAGE BOX LOCATIONS

There are no bear-proof food storage boxes on this route.

ROUTE DESCRIPTION

Mile 0 to 0.8 (Whitney Portal to North Fork Lone Pine Creek)
The trail starts immediately east of the Whitney Portal Store near several large Forest Service display signs. The first 0.8 mile follows the Mount Whitney Trail. This segment of the trail faces southwest and receives the full force of the hot summer sun. The trail begins by heading northeast, away from Whitney, but soon switchbacks toward the west and the crest of the Sierra Nevada. After about 0.5 mile, the trail crosses a small, unnamed stream. Continue up the trail to the next stream, the North Fork of Lone Pine Creek. The trail is gentle, gaining only 335 feet over 0.8 mile.

Mile 0.8 to 1.8
(North Fork Lone Pine Creek to Lower Boy Scout Lake)
Leave the Mount Whitney Trail before crossing the North Fork Lone Pine Creek. Here a well-used but unmaintained climber's trail ascends the

steep canyon. Over the next mile the trail gains 1600 feet until it reaches Lower Boy Scout Lake. The climber's trail is easily followed in most areas, but it occasionally disappears into thick brush or rocky talus slopes.

From the Mount Whitney Trail, follow the climber's trail for about 0.25 mile as it ascends the north side of the North Fork Lone Pine Creek. Cross the creek to its south side (near 9000 feet) and follow the climber's trail through the brush and talus for another 0.25 mile before crossing the stream a second time. Reach the base of the granite cliff and ascend the canyon along the toe of the precipice for about 100 feet. Leave the stream by turning right and ascending a short chimney containing a large tree about 40 feet up. Traverse east across rock ledges on the north side of the creek. These ledges are known as the Ebersbacher Ledges. Continue traversing east along these rock ledges until it is possible to climb up to the next level of ledges, turning back up stream heading west. The route stays on the north side (climber's right) of the creek to the outlet of Lower Boy Scout Lake, where it crosses to the south (left side).

Mile 1.8 to 2.7
(Lower Boy Scout Lake to Upper Boy Scout Lake)
The trail continues on the south side of the creek through talus, large boulders, and an occasional brush field. The trail gains 1000 feet in 0.9 mile. The route is steep but not nearly as steep as the segment below Lower Boy Scout Lake. From the upper end of Lower Boy Scout Lake, locate a gigantic boulder in the middle of a talus field several hundred feet above. Head for the boulder and cross under it and above the smaller boulder located just below. From this point, traverse right toward the creek through some brush. Near the creek, ascend smooth granite slabs situated between the brush fields and the creek. Gain several hundred feet on these granite slabs and then cross to the north side of the creek. Follow the climber's trail to Upper Boy Scout Lake, avoiding the willows and brush along the way.

Upper Boy Scout Lake makes an excellent camp. Camp at the lower end of the lake on the right or left side of the outlet stream.

If you plan to climb Mount Russell or Mount Carillon, leave the lower end of the lake and head northeast for about 0.25 mile. There are numerous use trails across the loose scree. Ascend the uppermost climber's trail. After crossing the obvious rock band, turn northwest

Climber descending Mount Russell (Routes 4 and 5)

up broad slopes of loose scree to the Russell–Carillon Pass at 13,300 feet. The loose scree can be discouraging. Kick steps in the scree just as you would when ascending a steep snow slope. This provides better footing and reduces the amount of backward slipping. From the pass, Mount Carillon is an easy Class 2 scramble to the top.

Mount Russell, on the other hand, is a challenging Class 3 climb along its exposed east ridge. From the Russell–Carillon Col the route looks difficult and appears to involve roped climbing in many places. Once you begin, the route is not nearly as difficult as it appears because many foot- and handholds are strategically placed along the route. My daughter, Sierra, at age 12 made the climb with some minor assistance and without a rope. The route passes over the east summit. Continue climbing along the ridge until you reach the main west summit at 14,088 feet. The climbing route lies either on the right (north side) of the east ridge or directly on top of the ridge. The ridge is about 0.65 mile long and takes at least 1.5 hours each way.

Mile 2.7 to 4.3
(Upper Boy Scout Lake to Whitney–Russell Col)
Above Upper Boy Scout Lake, the views of the great east face of Whitney and the four needles to the south of Whitney are magnificent. The route to Iceberg Lake passes below the near-vertical east face of Aiguille Extra (14,042 feet), Third Needle (14,107 feet), Crooks Peak (also

known as Day Needle; 14,173 feet), Keeler Needle (14,240 feet), and Mount Whitney (14,491 feet).

From the lower end of Upper Boy Scout Lake, hike south for about 0.25 mile, skirting the rock buttress, and then turn west, staying high above the unnamed lake to the south. There are numerous climber's trails in the area that ascend above the creek. The preferred route is to follow the lower trail that meets the creek near 11,900 feet. There are several excellent campsites along this route. Follow the drainage of the creek past a waterfall and main Iceberg Lake outlet creek (on your right). Continue beyond this waterfall and pass a wall of weeping water. Ascend easy ledges to the left of the last water. This will take you to the lower end of Iceberg Lake, located at the base of Whitney's sheer east face and the Mountaineers Route, the steep couloir to the right of the summit. Iceberg Lake is an impressive place to camp, relax, explore, and take photographs. From Iceberg Lake, technical rock climbers ascend various Class 5 routes on the east and southeast faces of Whitney. You may be able to see some roped climbers high on the rock face or others scrambling up the Mountaineers Route.

The unmaintained climber's trail continues to the Whitney–Russell Col, but it becomes more difficult to follow beyond Iceberg Lake. The route from Iceberg Lake over the Whitney–Russell Col and down the valley to Arctic Lakes is surprisingly gentle considering that it is sandwiched between the massive north face of Whitney and sheer Fishhook Arête of Mount Russell. Your senses will be on overload as you ascend the col and absorb the impressive sights and magnitude of these granite-faced peaks.

From Iceberg Lake, skirt the southwest side (left side) of the lake and ascend to the notch in the ridge above the lake. A faint climber's trail ascends to the pass. The Whitney–Russell Col is not the low point in the main ridge between Mounts Russell and Whitney but the notch in the ridge directly northwest of Iceberg Lake and immediately adjacent to the last buttress on the northeast ridge of Whitney. The low point in the Russell and Whitney ridge is above Upper Boy Scout Lake and contains Class 3 climbing on the east side.

Mile 4.3 to 6.5 (Whitney–Russell Col to Guitar Lake)
You pass from the John Muir Wilderness into the Sequoia National Park at the Whitney–Russell Col. From the Whitney–Russell Col,

descend easy slopes to the upper lake and follow the creek to Arctic Lakes. This seldom-visited valley is peaceful, relaxing, and gentle as it descends easy terrain to Guitar Lake and the John Muir Trail.

The creek flowing from Arctic Lakes continues its gentle descent to Guitar Lake. Select a campsite from many excellent sites along the creek 0.25 to 0.5 mile above Guitar Lake. There is a small unnamed tarn below Arctic Lakes with good camping at its lower end, or you can camp 0.25 mile below this small tarn on a flat bench near the creek at a remote campsite. A camp here will give you good views of Guitar Lake below and will keep you from the crowds on the John Muir Trail for one more night. Alternatively, hike down to the John Muir Trail and select a campsite near Guitar Lake. About 0.3 mile above Guitar Lake there are good campsites near a tarn at the 11,600-foot level and the 11,900-foot level. The 11,900-foot-level campsites are near a series of tarns linked by a small stream flowing toward Hitchcock Lakes. These excellent sites have rewarding views of Guitar Lake below and the impressive granite slopes of Mount Whitney above.

Mile 6.5 to 10 (Guitar Lake to Mount Whitney Trail)

From Guitar Lake, the John Muir Trail rises steadily for 3.5 miles and nearly 2000 feet up the steep west slopes of Whitney. A series of switchbacks seems endless but finally ends at the junction with the Mount Whitney Trail. The views of Hitchcock Lakes, Guitar Lake, and the mountain panorama improve as you gain elevation. The trail itself is impressive as it climbs through fields of talus, large rock faces, and striking granite towers. This segment of trail and the ninety-seven switchbacks below Trail Crest on the east side (Mount Whitney Trail, Route 6) are engineering marvels and tributes to the workers who built them. There are several large tent platforms at the John Muir–Mount Whitney Trail junction that can serve as campsites, but you must bring water because these are dry campsites.

Mile 10 to 12 (Mount Whitney Trail to Mount Whitney)

There are only 2 miles to the summit and a little more than 1000 feet of elevation gain. The most difficult hiking is over as the trail gradually reaches the highest point in the forty-eight contiguous United States. If you are not suffering from the altitude, the next 2 miles will be enjoyable as the trail snakes through impressive rock towers and past windows in the Sierra Nevada crest that provide breathtaking views of Trail Camp, the Mount Whitney Trail, and the Owens Valley far below. On the other hand, this may be the most strenuous portion of the trip because the altitude may have sucked the energy, strength, and desire from your body.

The trail along the west side of the crest leading to the summit of Whitney provides an excellent opportunity to climb Mount Muir, another 14,000-footer. It is a short 200-foot scramble to the top. To complete the Circumnavigation of Mount Whitney, hike down the Whitney Trail to Whitney Portal and the start of the trip. For complete details on the Mount Whitney Trail and a route description for Mount Muir, refer to Route 6.

Route 5: MOUNTAINEERS ROUTE

Trailhead ▲ Whitney Portal, 8365 feet
Rating ▲ Class 2 with a small amount of Class 3
Distance ▲ 4.7 miles to the summit
Elevation gain ▲ 6126 feet
Effort factor ▲ 8.5 hours
Trip duration ▲ 1–3 days
Maps ▲ Mount Whitney (1:24,000), Mount Whitney (1:62,500), or Tom Harrison Mount Whitney High Country Trail Map (1:63,360)

Trail Profile Table: Mountaineers Route

Milepost	Elevation (feet)	Elevation/ Mileage Change	Trail Grade (feet/miles)
Whitney Portal (0.0)	8,365	0.0/0.0	0.0
North Fork Lone Pine Creek (0.8)	8,700	335/0.8	419
Lower Boy Scout Lake (1.8)	10,300	1,600/1.0	1,600
Upper Boy Scout Lake (2.7)	11,300	1,000/0.9	1,111
Iceberg Lake (3.9)	12,600	1,300/1.2	1,083
Mount Whitney (4.7)	14,491	1,891/0.8	2,364

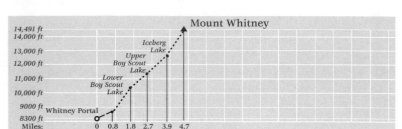

Trail Profile Graph: Mountaineers Route

IN A NUTSHELL

The Mountaineers Route is the distinctive couloir on the northeast face and right shoulder of Mount Whitney. It is readily seen from US 395 and the town of Lone Pine as well as from the Whitney Portal Road. In the winter and spring it is a challenging snow couloir for the ski mountaineer and backcountry snowboarder. In the summer and fall it is a rock scramble used by many climbers.

John Muir made the fifth ascent of Mount Whitney and the first ascent of what is today known as the Mountaineers Route in the fall of 1873. On foot, without a sleeping bag and modern equipment, Muir completed the round trip from Independence (not Lone Pine) to the summit of Whitney and back in just 4 days. Two years later he made another first ascent, that of Whitney's north slopes via the Whitney–Russell Col. After completing these climbs, John Muir wrote, "For climbers there is a canyon which comes down from the north shoulder of the Whitney peak. Well-seasoned limbs will enjoy the climb of 9,000 feet required for this direct route, but soft, succulent people should go the mule way." (In the 1800s the standard route up Whitney was from the west, i.e., the mule way.)

This is the most direct route to the summit of Mount Whitney. It is also the most technically difficult route included in this guidebook because there is a short section of Class 3 scrambling near the top of the Mountaineers Couloir. The couloir and the traverse across the north face may contain snow or ice throughout the summer and fall, so it is wise to take an ice ax and crampons. This exceptional route provides excellent views of the sheer granite east face of Whitney.

The route is rated Class 2, with a short Class 3 section near the top. The route includes 0.8 mile over the Whitney Trail (Class 1), 3.1

miles over an unmaintained climber's trail (Class 2), and 0.8 mile of scrambling up the Mountaineers Couloir (Class 2 with one section of Class 3) to the summit. Hikers with routefinding experience using a map and compass should be able to follow this challenging and rewarding route.

The Mountaineers Route ascends the couloir on the right.

Many complete this route in a single day, but it also makes a wonderful 2- or 3-day trip with the opportunity for a summit bid of Mount Russell as well.

This route also provides an excellent opportunity to traverse Mount Whitney by ascending the Mountaineers Route and descending the Mount Whitney Trail. However, a wilderness permit is required to descend the trail.

TRAILHEAD FACILITIES

The Whitney Portal Store and Cafe supplies basic meals, souvenirs, tee shirts, sweatshirts, books, maps, bear-proof canisters, showers (bring your own towel), and a cellular pay phone (bring money). There is a 10-unit hiker campground near the trailhead. There is also a picnic area with barbecue grills, tables, and a fishing pond. One mile to the east is a 44-unit campground with piped water and vault toilets.

HOW TO GET THERE

From the traffic light in Lone Pine on US 395, drive 13 miles west on the Whitney Portal Road to its end. The paved road usually is open from May to early November. In the winter the last 6 miles of the road are not plowed.

BEAR-PROOF WILDERNESS FOOD STORAGE BOX LOCATIONS

There are no bear-proof food storage boxes on this route.

ROUTE DESCRIPTION

Mile 0.0 to 0.8
(Whitney Portal to North Fork Lone Pine Creek)
Refer to Route 4 for the details of this trail segment.

Mile 0.8 to 1.8
(North Fork Lone Pine Creek to Lower Boy Scout Lake)
Refer to Route 4 for the details of this trail segment.

Mile 1.8 to 2.7
(Lower Boy Scout to Upper Boy Scout Lake)
Refer to Route 4 for the details of this trail segment and the route description to climb Mount Russell.

Mile 2.7 to 3.9 (Upper Boy Scout Lake to Iceberg Lake)
Refer to Route 4 for the details of this trail segment.

Mile 3.9 to 4.7 (Iceberg Lake to Mount Whitney)
The Mountaineers Route is the obvious couloir ascending the right shoulder of the east face of Whitney. In spring and early summer it is filled with snow. Crampons and an ice ax may be needed. Scramble to the top of the couloir that ends in a notch near 14,200 feet. The east ridge and east face of Mount Russell are impressive from the top of the couloir. Angle west, descending slightly, and then turn left toward the summit, climbing a gully that is extremely steep near the top, where a small segment of Class 3 climbing is encountered. This gully can also be icy any time of year. An alternative to this steep gully is to continue traversing west across the upper portion of the north face to the summit ridge. Once you have attained the ridge, follow the ridge for 5–10 minutes to the summit and the rock hut built by the Smithsonian Institution in 1909.

Retrace your steps down the Mountaineers Couloir, or if you did not leave any equipment or a camp below, you have the option of hiking out the Whitney Trail, but the route is twice as long. Refer to Route 6 for a complete description of the Mount Whitney Trail.

Route 6: MOUNT WHITNEY TRAIL

Trailhead ▲ Whitney Portal, 8365 feet
Rating ▲ Class 1
Distance ▲ 11 miles to the summit
Elevation gain ▲ 6306 feet
Effort factor ▲ 11.8 hours
Trip duration ▲ 1–3 days
Maps ▲ Mount Whitney (1:24,000), Mount Whitney (1:62,500), or Tom Harrison Mount Whitney High Country Trail Map (1:63,360)

Trail Profile Table: Mount Whitney Trail

Milepost	Elevation (feet)	Elevation/ Mileage Change	Trail Grade (feet/miles)
Whitney Portal (0.0)	8,365	0.0/0.0	0.0
Lone Pine Lake (2.8)	9,960	1,595/2.8	570
Outpost Camp (3.8)	10,360	400/1.0	400
Trail Camp (6.3)	12,040	1,680/2.5	672
Trail Crest (8.5)	13,660	1,620/2.2	736
John Muir Trail (9.0)	13,480	-180/0.5	-360
Mount Whitney (11.0)	14,491	1,011/2.0	506

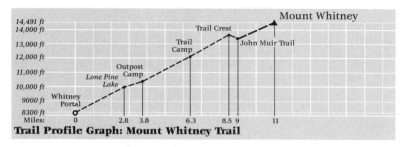

Trail Profile Graph: Mount Whitney Trail

IN A NUTSHELL

Just about anyone in good shape with a strong desire can complete the hike up Mount Whitney via the Mount Whitney Trail. A single-day climb (22-mile round trip) is out of the question for many, but a 2- or 3-day trip can be accomplished by most healthy and conditioned hikers. Altitude sickness caused by the rapid rise in elevation is a serious deterrent for many. Driving from near sea level to more than 8000 feet at Whitney Portal and then ascending to 12,000 or 14,000 feet in a day may be too rapid for many hikers. This can usually be overcome by spending one night at the Whitney Portal Campground (8000 feet) or camping one or two nights at Outpost Camp (10,360 feet) or Trail Camp (12,000 feet). This allows your body to adjust to the altitude and the lack of oxygen at these higher elevations. Based on records from the Sequoia National Park and the Inyo National Forest, it appears that only about 33 percent of those attempting the peak reach the summit. Altitude sickness is a main contributor to the 67 percent failure rate.

The Mount Whitney Trail is the most heavily used route to the summit, with about 24,000 persons securing a permit for the trail during 2000 (see Appendix 6). The route follows an excellent trail all the way to the summit and so is rated as Class 1. However, in the spring and early summer there may be snow on the steep slopes between Trail Camp and Trail Crest. In this situation, crampons and an ice ax may be necessary. Contact the Forest Service District Office in Lone Pine for trail conditions.

If attempting the summit in a single day, refer to the suggestions in Chapter 4. When planning a climb, it is difficult to predict how long it will take, but it is not unusual for a round trip to the summit and back to take 12–18 hours (8–12 hours for the ascent and 4–6 hours for the descent). An early, predawn start is necessary to summit and return in a single day.

The Mount Whitney Trail–John Muir Trail winds through the rock towers on the west side of the crest. This photo was taken about 1 mile from the summit of Mount Whitney.

TRAILHEAD FACILITIES

The Whitney Portal Store and Cafe supplies basic meals, souvenirs, tee shirts, sweatshirts, books, maps, bear-proof canisters, showers (bring your own towel), and a cellular pay phone. There is a 10-unit hiker campground near the trailhead. There is a picnic area with barbecue grills, tables, and a fishing pond near the store. One mile to the east is a forty-four–unit campground with piped water and vault toilets.

HOW TO GET THERE

From the signal light in Lone Pine on US 395, drive 13 miles west on the Whitney Portal Road to its end. The paved road usually is open from May to early November. In the winter the last 6 miles of the road are not plowed.

BEAR-PROOF WILDERNESS FOOD STORAGE BOX LOCATIONS

There are no bear-proof food storage boxes on this route.

ROUTE DESCRIPTION

Mile 0 to 2.8 (Whitney Portal to Lone Pine Lake)
The Mount Whitney Trail starts immediately east of the Whitney Portal Store near several large Forest Service wilderness display signs. This segment of the trail faces southwest and receives the full force of the hot summer sun. An early morning start will help you avoid the heat. The trail begins by heading northeast, away from Mount Whitney, but soon switchbacks toward the west and the crest of the Sierra Nevada. After about 0.5 mile, the trail crosses a small, unnamed stream. At 0.8 mile the North Fork of Lone Pine Creek is crossed, and just beyond the creek crossing the trail enters the John Muir Wilderness.

After entering the wilderness area, the trail begins a series of switchbacks through a brushy area of chinquapin oak, mountain mahogany, and chaparral. To the left is Lone Pine Creek cascading down a series of steep drops as it flows from Lone Pine Lake. After many switchbacks and about 2 miles of steady climbing, the trail levels off slightly. Just before reaching the trail junction to Lone Pine

Lake, the trail crosses a small stream. It is a short walk to the beautiful Lone Pine Lake, perched on a glacial bench overlooking Whitney Portal and the Owens Valley.

Mile 2.8 to 3.8 (Lone Pine Lake to Outpost Camp)

The brush of the lower trail segment is supplanted by a healthy forest consisting mainly of foxtail pine, limber pine, Jeffrey pine, and lodgepole pine. Over the next mile the trail gradually gains 400 feet in elevation. As the trail approaches Bighorn Park, it drops down slightly, skirts the meadow, and crosses the stream several times before reaching Outpost Camp located at the far end of Bighorn Park. Bighorn Park is a large meadow area covered with willows. Lone Pine Creek runs through the meadow and forms a scenic waterfall that is located at the upper edge of the meadow.

Outpost Camp and Trail Camp are the two designated areas for camping along the Mount Whitney Trail. The Forest Service has placed a solar toilet at the upper end of Outpost Camp. Please use the facility. From Outpost Camp there is still more than 4000 feet and roughly 7 miles to the summit. Because of the heavy usage of Trail Camp and the corresponding downstream sanitation problems, make sure you carefully treat the water at both Trail Camp and Outpost Camp. Although Trail Camp is the best choice for a base camp, on your return trip, consider bypassing Trail Camp and spending your last night at Outpost Camp. Trail Camp is overused and generally crowded.

Mile 3.8 to 6.3 (Outpost Camp to Trail Camp)

Over the next 2.5 miles the trail gains nearly 1700 feet to 12,040 feet at Trail Camp. The scenery and vistas along this segment of trail are exceptional. As you leave Outpost Camp, the sheer granite face of Thor Peak dominates the view. Mirror Lake lies in a lovely glacial cirque at the base of Thor Peak, 0.5 mile beyond Outpost Camp. Mirror Lake makes a beautiful rest stop but is closed to camping. At one time this was a popular spot to camp, but it was overused, causing serious damage to the fragile lake and meadow environments.

Above the Mirror Lake cirque, the trail ascends a series of switchbacks. The trail levels off for a short distance, crossing polished granite slabs as the trail reaches the tree line. Here there are exceptional views of Mirror Lake, Wotans Throne, Thor Peak, and Mount

Irvine. From Mirror Lake climb 800 feet over 1 mile to the small but picturesque Trailside Meadow situated at 11,400 feet. No camping is permitted here, but it makes for a nice place to take a breather. From Trailside Meadow it is another mile and a 600-foot climb to Trail Camp. As you ascend the trail, the scenic vistas become more expansive with views of Consultation Lake, Arc Pass, Mount McAdie, Mount Muir, and the great east face of the Sierra Nevada.

Trail Camp is the logical location for a base camp, but it is nearly an ecological disaster. Too many people in a confined area have ad-

The Mount Whitney Trail provides many fabulous views such as this one near Outpost Camp.

versely affected the fragile environment. A solar toilet, erected some years ago by the Forest Service, helps with the disposal of solid human waste, but it cannot handle the large demand of hikers and overnight campers and must be shut down periodically. When the solar toilet is closed, it is only a slight exaggeration to say that human waste and toilet paper are under practically every movable rock in the camping area. Of course, the runoff from all this waste seeps into the nearby lake and stream. The lake at Trail Camp is thriving with algae growth fed by nutrients from all the improperly disposed-of human waste. This is in stark contrast to a typical 12,000-foot alpine lake, which is clear, clean, and devoid of algae growth.

A word of caution is warranted. Do not fill your water bottles from the nearby lake at Trail Camp. Boiling, filtering, or treating the water with purification tablets may provide adequate safeguards but higher quality water is nearby. Walk to the upper end of the lake and hike up the inlet stream a safe distance. Fill your water bottles from the stream flowing into the lake. Alternatively, hike up the main trail towards the ninety-seven switchbacks and fill your water bottles at a point as close to the snow as possible. Both are much better sources of water than the lake.

Paradoxically, Trail Camp is the last reliable place to get water. Make sure your water bottles are full for the hike to the summit.

Mile 6.3 to 8.5 (Trail Camp to Trail Crest)

Trail Camp is located above Consultation Lake and at the base of the great east face of the Sierra Nevada. The 14,000-foot Mount Muir is due west and clearly visible from the camp. Mount Whitney is far to the north (right) just out of view. From Trail Camp, the trail ascends 96, 97, 98, or 99 (depending on the count) switchbacks up a narrow granite buttress to Trail Crest and the boundary of Sequoia National Park. Some years ago the trail continued farther to the west before ascending steep slopes to the crest. Because the snow does not readily melt out from this area each year, the trail was moved to its current location so that it would be clear of snow for a longer time each summer and fall. The trail is not particularly steep but is unrelenting in its climb to the crest, gaining 1620 feet in 2.2 miles, or 736 feet per mile.

You enter Sequoia National Park at the crest. Here you are greeted with awesome views of Sequoia National Park to the west and north.

The park stretches as far as the eye can see and beyond. Immediately below are the beautiful Hitchcock Lakes and Guitar Lake. Beyond these lakes are the Great Western Divide and the Kaweah mountains.

Mile 8.5 to 9 (Trail Crest to the John Muir Trail)

The trail drops slightly from 13,660 to 13,480 feet to meet the John Muir Trail. The John Muir Trail, originating in Yosemite Valley about 223 miles to the north, passes Crabtree Meadow and Guitar Lake as it ascends the west slopes of Whitney on its way to the summit. There are several large tent platforms near the trail intersection. These campsites are dry, so bring plenty of water if you plan to camp here.

Mile 9 to 11 (John Muir Trail to Mount Whitney)

There are only 2 miles to the summit and a little more than 1000 feet of elevation gain. The most difficult hiking is over as the John Muir Trail gradually reaches the highest point in the Lower 48. If you are not suffering from the altitude, the next 2 miles will be extremely rewarding as the trail snakes through impressive rock towers and past windows in the Sierra Nevada crest that provide breathtaking views of Trail Camp, the Mount Whitney Trail, and the Owens Valley far below. On the other hand, this may be the most strenuous portion of the trip because the altitude may have sucked the strength, energy, and desire from your body.

The trail along the west side of the crest provides an excellent opportunity to scramble up Mount Muir and to bag any of the four 14,000-foot subpeaks of Mount Whitney: Aiguille Extra, Third Needle, Crooks Peak (also known as Day Needle), and Keeler Needle. Each of these subpeaks is only a couple hundred feet above the John Muir Trail. From the junction of the Mount Whitney Trail and the John Muir Trail, ascend the two switchbacks in the trail and proceed to a large rock cairn marking the cutoff to Mount Muir. The summit of Mount Muir is visible from this point. Ascend a shallow gully of loose scree and head toward the notch in the ridge to the right of the main summit. From this notch angle left and climb a small chimney. Traverse left across a sloping ledge. Climb a crack to your right, gaining the small summit block. There is room for only three or four carefully placed climbers on the top at any one time. The top 50 feet is easy Class 3. From the summit there are impressive views of the east face of Mount Muir directly below, ninety-seven switchbacks in the Mount Whitney Trail, Trail Camp, Consultation Lake, Arc Pass, Whitney Portal, and the Owens Valley far below.

To ascend any of the four 14,000-foot subpeaks of Whitney, leave the John Muir Trail and scramble up the west slopes to the summit of these needles. All are easy Class 2 scrambles and provide a bird's-eye view of the sheer, near-vertical east face. The top of each needle is visible from the trail. To reach the first needle, Aiguille Extra, leave the John Muir Trail about 1 mile beyond the junction of the Mount Whitney Trail and scramble to the top. The others follow in quick succession. For the last and highest needle, Keeler Needle, leave the trail just before it turns west heading away from the crest to begin the final climb to the summit of Whitney.

Congratulations, you have made it to the highest point in California and the contiguous forty-eight states. Sign the summit register and take pictures of your historic moment. From the summit you will be greeted with impressive views of Mount Langley and Mount Muir to the south; the Kaweah Range and Sawtooth Peak to the west; Mount Russell, Tulainyo Lake (to the right of Mount Russell), the highest large alpine lake in the Sierra Nevada, Mount Williamson, Milestone Mountain, Table Mountain, Thunder Mountain, and Mount Brewer to the north; and Trail Camp, Mount Whitney Trail switchbacks, Consultation Lake, Arc Pass, and Owens Valley to the east. If the weather is nice, spend some time on top; take in the scenery and savor your accomplishment.

Route 7: MEYSAN LAKE ROUTE

Trailhead ▲ Whitney Portal Campground, 8000 feet

Rating ▲ Class 2

Distance ▲ 12.1 miles to the summit

Elevation gain ▲ 8971 feet

Effort factor ▲ 15.1 hours

Trip duration ▲ 4–6 days

Maps ▲ Mount Whitney and Mount Langley (1:24,000), Mount Whitney and Lone Pine (1:62,500), or Tom Harrison Mount Whitney High Country Trail Map (1:63,360)

Trail Profile Table: Meysan Lake Route

Milepost	Elevation (feet)	Elevation/ Mileage Change	Trail Grade (feet/miles)
Whitney Portal Campground (0.0)	8,000	0.0/0.0	0.0
Grass Lake (3.8)	10,900	2,900/3.8	763
Meysan Lake (5.0)	11,500	600/1.2	500
LeConte–Mallory Pass (6.0)	13,500	2,000/1.0	2,000
Sky-Blue Lake (7.0)	11,600	-1,900/1.0	-1,900
Crabtree Pass (8.6)	12,560	960/1.6	600
Upper Crabtree Lake (8.8)	12,160	-400/0.2	-2,000
Trail Crest (9.6)	13,660	1,500/0.8	1,875
John Muir Trail (10.1)	13,480	-180/0.5	-360
Mount Whitney (12.1)	14,491	1,011/2.0	506

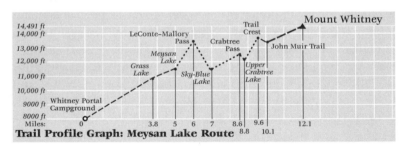

Trail Profile Graph: Meysan Lake Route

IN A NUTSHELL

This strenuous route starts by ascending the steep trail to Meysan Lake. From the lake, the route ascends through steep and loose scree to the LeConte–Mallory Pass at 13,500 feet, drops down to the impressive Sky-Blue Lake (one of the most beautiful spots in the entire Sierra Nevada), and crosses Crabtree Pass on its way to Trail Crest and the summit of Mount Whitney. The crux of this route is the 2000-foot climb from Meysan Lake (11,500 feet) to the high plateau and the LeConte–Mallory Pass (13,500 feet). Once you reach the pass, it is easy hiking over gentle terrain to Sky-Blue Lake. From Sky-Blue Lake, the Meysan Lake Route follows the same course used by Route 8 (New Army Pass Route).

The route is rated Class 2 because it includes 7.5 miles over maintained trails (Class 1) and 4.6 miles of cross-country travel (Class 2), of which 1 mile is over steep terrain that is not technically difficult but is strenuous. This is a difficult but rewarding route. You can easily obtain a wilderness permit reservation for the Meysan Lake Route because the quota for the trail is seldom reached. Request permission to enter the Mount Whitney Zone when you secure your permit.

TRAILHEAD FACILITIES

A 44-unit campground (Whitney Portal Campground) with piped water and vault toilets is located at the trailhead. One mile to the west, near the start of the Mount Whitney Trail, the Whitney Portal Store and Cafe supplies basic meals, souvenirs, tee shirts, sweatshirts, books, maps, bear-proof canisters, showers (bring your own towel), and a cellular pay phone. There is a 10-unit hiker campground, picnic area with barbecue grills and tables, and a fishing pond near the store.

HOW TO GET THERE

From the US 395 signal light in Lone Pine, drive west for 12 miles on the Whitney Portal Road to the Whitney Portal Campground, located 1 mile east of the end of the road. Park on the left side of the road. The paved road usually is open from May to early November. In the winter the last 6 miles of the road are not plowed.

BEAR-PROOF WILDERNESS FOOD STORAGE BOX LOCATIONS

There are no bear-proof food storage boxes on this route.

ROUTE DESCRIPTION

Mile 0 to 3.8 (Whitney Portal Campground to Grass Lake)
Park along the Whitney Portal Road, near the Meysan Lake trail sign. Walk through the Whitney Portal Campground, following the signs that direct you along a combination of trails and roads past the beautiful summer cabins perched on the steep mountainside. The elevation gain along the trail is continuous and the switchbacks are unrelenting as the trail ascends the canyon at nearly 800 feet per

The route follows these rock and snow gullies above Meysan Lake to the pass near Mount Mallory. Mount LeConte is on the left.

mile. The trail is located on the sunny side of the canyon, so it may be a warm hike in the afternoon. The route of the trail is impressive, with the northwest face of Lone Pine Peak towering over the canyon on your left and sheer granite walls rising on your right.

Mile 3.8 to 5 (Grass Lake to Meysan Lake)

Grass Lake is not readily visible from the trail, but you can follow a short spur trail to the small lake. From this junction, the main trail turns right and climbs above Grass Lake on its way to Camp Lake. Camp Lake is a beautiful tarn located near a small meadow. As one might surmise from the lake's name, this is a favorite place for families and fishers to camp. Do not camp here; push on to Meysan Lake by skirting the right shore of Camp Lake, following the creek to Meysan Lake. This is the route of an old 1940s and 1950s trail to Meysan Lake. An ancient sign and sections of the old trail are visible as one quickly ascends to Meysan Lake.

Meysan Lake makes an ideal campsite for the first night. This will provide your party with a fresh start the following morning for the tedious and sometimes discouraging climb of the loose scree gullies above the lake. The crux of the entire trip is this 2000-foot ascent above Meysan Lake to the high plateau and pass above.

Mile 5 to 6 (Meysan Lake to LeConte–Mallory Pass)

The large Meysan Lake basin is ringed, from right to left, by the four impressive summits of Mount Irvine, Mount Mallory, Mount LeConte, and Lone Pine Peak. On the right, the base of the vertical granite face of Mount Irvine rises from near the shore of Meysan Lake. In the center, the large glacial basin above Meysan Lake is split by the rugged east ridge of Mount Mallory.

To the left of the east ridge of Mount Mallory are four distinctive couloirs that ascend to the LeConte–Mallory Plateau. The best way to reach the LeConte–Mallory Pass is to ascend the third or fourth couloir (the two on the far right). These are usually filled with snow late into the summer. Using a snow route allows you to avoid the loose scree that is so tedious to climb. Crampons and ice ax are needed to ascend the hard snow. If you do not bring crampons, an alternative route is to ascend the second couloir. Where the second couloir steepens and downsloping slabs are encountered, traverse right along natural ledges to the rib dividing the second couloir from the snow-filled third couloir. Follow this rib to the plateau. The footing along the rib is loose but generally somewhat better than that found in the gullies. This 1-mile section is the crux of the route and is strenuous but is soon passed.

Once the LeConte–Mallory plateau is attained, the correct pass is the low point on the far right near the base of Mount Mallory. From the pass, it is an easy scramble to the summit of Mount Mallory.

Mile 6 to 7 (LeConte–Mallory Pass to Sky-Blue Lake)

From the pass south of Mount Mallory, descend toward the unnamed lake due south of Arc Pass and then on to Sky-Blue Lake. The hiking is over easy terrain. You are approaching one of the most beautiful areas of the entire Sierra Nevada: Rock Creek and Sky-Blue Lake, with the surrounding sheer granite faces of Mount Pickering and Mount Newcomb. The rock faces above Sky-Blue Lake are particularly inspiring as the sunrise casts a golden glow on the towering cliffs above. There are excellent campsites at Sky-Blue Lake, or you can continue on to the next lake just below Mount McAdie's south face and camp.

Mile 7 to 8.6 (Sky-Blue Lake to Crabtree Pass)

The route to Crabtree Pass (12,560 feet) is a short and enjoyable hike over moderately difficult terrain. The alpine environment is exceptional and includes meadows, wildflowers, granite bluffs, lake basins, cascading streams, and brilliant blue sky, all framed by the sheer granite walls of Mount McAdie (on the right) and Mount Newcomb (on the left). From Sky-Blue Lake, head north following one of the streams that flows into the lake. Pass by the large unnamed lake near 12,200 feet and ascend 400 feet to the notch (Crabtree Pass) located to the left (southwest) of Mount McAdie.

Mile 8.6 to 8.8 (Crabtree Pass to Upper Crabtree Lake)

Descend 400 feet to the upper lake in the Crabtree basin. The descent is steep, with several bluffs that can be avoided or descended easily (Class 2).

Mile 8.8 to 9.6 (Upper Crabtree Lake to Trail Crest)

Ascending the loose, decomposed granite sand above Upper Crabtree Lake is tiring as one steps forward and then slips back in the soft sand. It is particularly laborious with a full pack in the hot sun. Kick steps in the soft scree just as you would climbing a steep snow slope. Angle up toward Discovery Pinnacle and crest the ridge to the right (southeast) of Discovery Pinnacle. Traverse under Discovery Pinnacle (on the Mount Whitney Trail side) and hike along the ridge for a short distance before dropping down to the Mount Whitney Trail immediately below.

Mile 9.6 to 12.1 (Trail Crest to Mount Whitney)

Drop your pack and head for the summit by following the trail to the top. For a description of this last trail segment, refer to Route 6. After summiting, return to your pack and hike out the Mount Whitney Trail (see Route 6 for a description of the trail). If you plan to hike back out via Meysan Lake or over New Army Pass, hustle back to your camp at Sky-Blue Lake.

ROUTE 8: NEW ARMY PASS ROUTE

Trailhead ▲ Horseshoe Meadow, 10,040 feet

Rating ▲ Class 2

Distance ▲ 18.1 miles to the summit

Elevation gain ▲ 6751 feet

Effort factor ▲ 15.9 hours

Trip duration ▲ 4–6 days

Maps ▲ Cirque Peak, Mount Whitney, and Mount Langley (1:24,000); Mount Whitney and Olancha (1:62,500); or Tom Harrison Mount Whitney High Country Trail Map (1:63,360)

Trail Profile Table: New Army Pass Route

Milepost	Elevation (feet)	Elevation/ Mileage Change	Trail Grade (feet/miles)
Horseshoe Meadow (0.0)	10,040	0.0/0.0	0.0
Cottonwood Lakes Basin (4.0)	11,000	1,160/4.0	290
New Army Pass (7.0)	12,320	1,320/3.0	440
Soldier Lakes (10.5)	10,800	-1,520/3.5	-434
Sky-Blue Lake (13.0)	11,600	800/2.5	320
Crabtree Pass (14.6)	12,560	960/1.6	600
Upper Crabtree Lake (14.8)	12,160	-400/0.2	-2,000
Trail Crest (15.6)	13,660	1,500/0.8	1,875
John Muir Trail (16.1)	13,480	-180/0.5	-360
Mount Whitney (18.1)	14,491	1,011/2.0	506

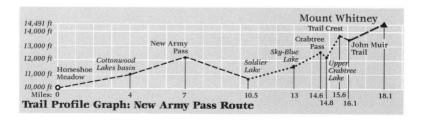

Trail Profile Graph: New Army Pass Route

Map 7: Routes 8 and 9

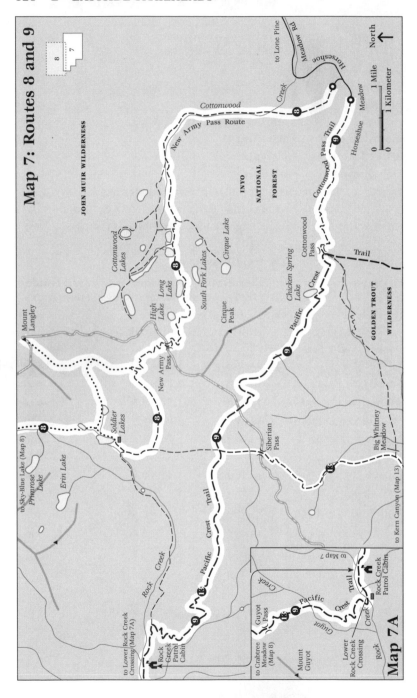

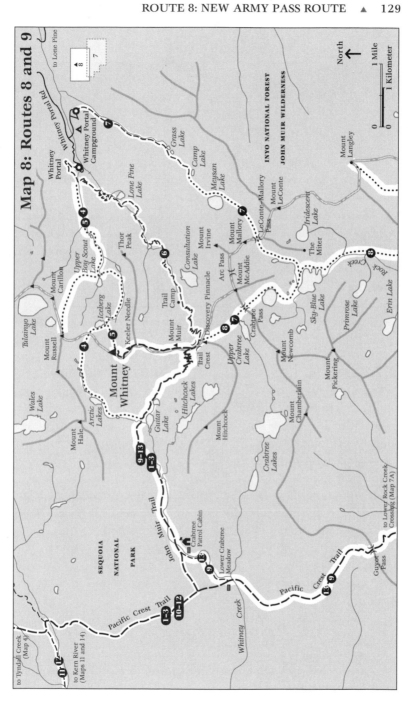

Map 8: Routes 8 and 9

to Lone Pine

to Lone Pine

North

1 Mile

1 Kilometer

Whitney Portal Rd

Whitney Portal

Whitney Portal Campground

Grass Lake

Camp Lake

Meysan Lake

INYO NATIONAL FOREST

JOHN MUIR WILDERNESS

Mount Langley

Lone Pine Lake

Mount Carillon

Upper Boy Scout Lake

Thor Peak

Consultation Lake

Mount Irvine

LeConte-Mallory Pass

Mount LeConte

Iridescent Lake

The Miter

Talainyo Lake

Mount Russell

Iceberg Lake

Keeler Needle

Arc Pass

Mount McAddie

Rock Creek

Wales Lake

Arctic Lakes

Mount Muir

Discovery Pinnacle

Crabtree Pass

Sky-Blue Lake

Primrose Lake

Erin Lake

Mount Hale

Guitar Lake

Trail Crest

Upper Crabtree Lake

Mount Newcomb

Mount Pickering

Hitchcock Lakes

Mount Hitchcock

Mount Chamberlain

Crabtree Lakes

Mount Whitney

Trail Camp

SEQUOIA NATIONAL PARK

John Muir Trail

Crabtree Patrol Cabin

Lower Crabtree Meadow

Pacific Crest Trail

Guyot Pass

to Lower Rock Creek Crossing (Map 7A)

to Tyndall Creek (Map 4)

to Kern River (Maps 11 and 14)

Pacific Crest Trail

Whitney Creek

Pacific Crest Trail

IN A NUTSHELL

Named for the cottonwood trees that were located at the original trailhead in the Owens Valley, the Cottonwood Lakes–New Army Pass trail provides access to the southern portion of the John Muir Wilderness, Sequoia National Park, and Mount Whitney via Rock Creek. Cottonwood Lakes are home to the golden trout, California's state fish.

This excellent route skirts the Cottonwood Lakes basin; ascends New Army Pass; follows the impressive Rock Creek drainage beneath the spectacular granite faces of Joe Devel Peak, Mount Pickering, and Mount Newcomb; passes by the beautiful Sky-Blue Lake; and crosses Crabtree Pass on its way to Trail Crest and the summit of Whitney. The route also provides an excellent opportunity to climb Mount Langley (Class 2), another 14,000-footer in the Whitney region. Mount Langley was first climbed in 1871 by Clarence King, who mistakenly thought he was making the first successful ascent of Whitney.

This route includes 5.1 miles of cross-country travel (Class 2) and 13 miles over maintained trails (Class 1). Hikers with routefinding experience using a map and compass should be able to follow this superb route. The route is not technically difficult: my daughter, Sierra, completed this route at age 10, climbing Cirque Peak by moonlight on the first day, Mount Langley on the second day, and Whitney on the third day. This is an enjoyable and rewarding route. An added bonus is that it avoids the crowded Mount Whitney Trail for much of the way. The route finishes by descending the Whitney Trail to Whitney Portal. This route and Routes 4 and 11 are my favorites.

If you do not plan to climb Mount Langley or Cirque Peak, an alternative route is to take the Cottonwood Pass Trail (Route 9) to Lower Soldier Lake and follow Route 8 from this point.

The drive and rapid rise to 10,000 feet can cause a hiker to be lethargic with mountain sickness the first day. Spending a day and night at the Horseshoe Meadow campground is helpful in adjusting to the altitude.

TRAILHEAD FACILITIES

There are twelve excellent walk-in campground sites, toilets, and piped water near the trailhead.

HOW TO GET THERE

From the traffic light in Lone Pine on US 395, drive 3.5 miles west on the Whitney Portal Road. Turn south (left) onto Horseshoe Meadow Road and continue 20.5 miles to Horseshoe Meadow. Just before the end of the road, turn right and proceed 0.3 mile to the Cottonwood Lakes and New Army Pass trailhead (not to be confused with the Cottonwood Pass trailhead). The paved road usually is open from May to late October.

BEAR-PROOF WILDERNESS FOOD STORAGE BOX LOCATIONS

▲ **Lower Soldier Lake:** A long, narrow meadow is located south of the lake along the lake's outlet stream. One box is located on the east side of this meadow about 600 feet south of the lake.

ROUTE DESCRIPTION

Mile 0 to 4
(Horseshoe Meadow to Cottonwood Lakes Basin)
Over the first 2 miles, the trail gradually drops about 200 feet, crosses a creek, and then regains the lost elevation. The trail turns west and begins a moderate climb of 900 feet, over the next 2 miles, as it gains the Cottonwood Lakes basin. The Cottonwood Lakes basin is home to the golden trout and is a favorite among fishers. Along the way are several trail junctions; always take the trail heading for New Army Pass.

Mile 4 to 7 (Cottonwood Lakes Basin to New Army Pass)
Continue hiking west, skirting the Cottonwood Lakes basin past Long Lake and High Lake. These lakes are situated at the foot of the south ridge of Mount Langley and directly below New Army Pass. There is an impressive sheer granite face rising to the north of High Lake. At High Lake the trail begins its nearly 1000-foot ascent to New Army Pass. Camp at Long Lake (in the trees) or High Lake (above the tree line) or push on to New Army Pass. As you near the pass, the unique beehive-like rock formations of New Army Pass come into view. Cross over New Army Pass and hike about 15 minutes down the other side over gentle terrain to where the trail crosses a wash and a spring. This is a good place to camp when water is available. The wash and spring usually have water in the summer but by fall may have dried up.

This high campsite provides great views as the sun sets in the west over the Coast Range. It also affords a wonderful opportunity to climb both Cirque Peak and Mount Langley. The climbing is not technically difficult, but you may feel the altitude as you ascend Mount Langley's 14,022-foot slopes.

To climb Mount Langley from the wash, ascend an ill-defined ridge by passing to the left of several prominent rocks on the ridge. Continue traversing gentle slopes, gaining elevation gradually. There will be a broad valley on your left. Head toward a red, sandy saddle (12,400 feet) at the head of this valley. Drop your pack and climb decomposed granite sandy slopes to the summit (Class 2). There are numerous use trails ascending the south slopes of Mount Langley. The most difficult part of the climb is the frustration of stepping up and then sliding back in the loose sand. From the summit you will have wonderful views of Cirque Peak and Olancha Peak to the south, and of course Mount Muir and Mount Whitney, 5 miles to the north, along with hundreds of other peaks in all directions.

Return to your pack at the red, sandy saddle. Here you can follow a use trail heading west. Descend toward the large Upper Soldier Lake and continue toward Lower Soldier Lake. Before reaching the lower lake, you will see a distinctive notch or gap in the rugged granite in which the lower lake's inlet stream flows. Hike through the notch, following the stream to the small tarn located at the western base of the nose of the Major General. From this tarn, just above 11,200 feet, traverse into Rock Creek following use trails to Sky-Blue Lake.

High Lake and the cliffs near New Army Pass

Mile 7 to 10.5 (New Army Pass to Lower Soldier Lake)

If you do not plan to ascend Mount Langley, stay on the New Army Pass Route. Pass the spring and wash northwest of New Army Pass and follow the trail for 2.5 miles to the Siberian Pass Trail. The trail drops steeply, losing nearly 1500 feet in 2.5 miles.

At the junction with the Siberian Pass Trail, turn right (north) toward Rock Creek and Lower Soldier Lake. In 0.7 mile, cross the creek and take the right fork in the trail to Lower Soldier Lake. The lake is tucked away under the southwest slopes of the Major General. A bear-proof food storage box is located on a rocky peninsula on the south side of the lake. Hike around the right shore to reach the bear-proof box.

Mile 10.5 to 13 (Lower Soldier Lake to Sky-Blue Lake)

Hike to the upper end of Lower Soldier Lake. Ascend the lake's inlet stream, angling left through a distinctive gap in the steep granite. Follow the stream through this gap to the small tarn at the western base of the Major General. Traverse into Rock Creek drainage at 11,200 feet. Rock Creek and its surroundings are magnificent as the creek snakes between Mount Langley, Mount LeConte, and Mount McAdie to the east and the impressive wall formed by the summits of Joe Devel, Pickering, and Newcomb to the west. Follow Rock Creek and an old use trail over easy terrain to Sky-Blue Lake. The rock faces above Sky-Blue Lake are particularly photogenic as early-morning sunrises cast a golden glow on the towering cliffs. There are excellent campsites at Sky-Blue Lake, or you can continue to the next lake just below Mount McAdie's south face and camp.

An alternative to the gap route above Lower Soldier Lake is to hike down the trail to Lower Rock Creek Lake. About 200 yards before Rock Creek Trail crosses Rock Creek, turn right onto an unsigned use trail. This option is a couple of miles longer and also leads to Sky-Blue Lake.

Mile 13 to 14.6 (Sky-Blue Lake to Crabtree Pass)

The route to Crabtree Pass (12,560 feet) is a short and enjoyable hike over moderate terrain. The alpine environment is exceptional and includes meadows, wildflowers, granite bluffs, lake basins, cascading streams, and brilliant blue sky, all framed by the sheer granite walls of Mount McAdie and Mount Newcomb. From Sky-Blue Lake, head north following one of the streams that flows into the lake. Pass by the large unnamed lake near 12,200 feet and ascend 400 feet to the notch to the left (southwest) of Mount McAdie.

Mile 14.6 to 14.8 (Crabtree Pass to Upper Crabtree Lake)

Descend 400 feet to the upper lake in the Crabtree basin. The descent is steep, with several bluffs that can be avoided easily (Class 2).

Mile 14.8 to 15.6 (Upper Crabtree Lake to Trail Crest)

This is the least desirable portion of the route; climbing the loose, decomposed granite sand is exceedingly tedious as one steps forward and then slips back in the soft sand. It is particularly laborious with a full pack in the hot sun. Kick steps in the soft scree just as you would when climbing steep, firm snow. Angle up toward Discovery Pinnacle and crest the ridge to the right (southeast) of Discovery Pinnacle. Traverse under Discovery Pinnacle (above the Mount Whitney Trail) and hike along the ridge for a short distance before dropping down to the Mount Whitney Trail immediately below. It is only 100 feet to Trail Crest.

Mile 15.6 to 18.1 (Trail Crest to Mount Whitney)

Drop your pack and head for the summit. After summiting, return to your pack and hike out the Mount Whitney Trail (see Route 6 for a description). If you plan to hike out via New Army Pass, hustle back to your camp at Sky-Blue Lake.

Route 9: COTTONWOOD PASS TRAIL

Trailhead　▲　Horseshoe Meadow, 9920 feet
Rating　▲　Class 1
Distance　▲　29.7 miles to the summit
Elevation gain　▲　7341 feet
Effort factor　▲　22.2 hours
Trip duration　▲　4–6 days
Maps　▲　Mount Whitney and Cirque Peak (1:24,000), Mount Whitney and Kern Peak (1:62,500), or Tom Harrison Mount Whitney High Country Trail Map (1:63,360)

Trail Profile Table: Cottonwood Pass Trail

Milepost	Elevation (feet)	Elevation/ Mileage Change	Trail Grade (feet/miles)
Horseshoe Meadow (0.0)	9,920	0.0/0.0	0.0
Cottonwood Pass (3.5)	11,180	1,260/3.5	360
Siberian Pass Trail (8.1)	11,040	560/4.6	up/down
Lower Rock Creek Crossing (14.0)	9,520	-1,520/5.9	-258
Guyot Pass (16.8)	10,880	1,360/2.8	486
Lower Crabtree Meadow (20.4)	10,330	-550/3.6	-153
Guitar Lake (24.2)	11,500	1,170/3.8	308
Mount Whitney Trail (27.7)	13,480	1,980/3.5	566
Mount Whitney (29.7)	14,491	1,011/2.0	506

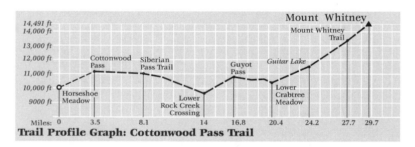

Trail Profile Graph: Cottonwood Pass Trail

IN A NUTSHELL

This popular trail is perhaps the easiest of the routes not originating at Whitney Portal. This trailhead (along with the New Army Pass trailhead) starts at nearly 10,000 feet, the highest starting point of any of the trips in this guidebook, with an elevation gain of only 7341 feet over about 30 miles of trail. The route begins by ascending Cottonwood Pass (a gradual climb of about 1260 feet), where it picks up the Pacific Crest Trail traversing the southwest slopes of Cirque Peak. From the Sierra Nevada crest, the Pacific Crest Trail descends 1500 feet to Rock Creek before starting a climb of 1360 feet to Guyot Pass. From the pass the trail advances past Crabtree Meadow and the

Crabtree Patrol Cabin, where it joins the John Muir Trail on its way to the summit of Whitney.

This trail is a good choice for an early season ascent. Because of its southerly route and sun-drenched terrain, it is the earliest of the trails in this guidebook to open in the spring. It is essentially free of snow by mid-June, so it is a good trail to take before the wilderness permit quotas become effective each summer (starting the last Friday by June). Refer to Chapter 4 for a complete discussion of wilderness permit requirements.

The route is splendid in the early hiking season of June and July

Cirque Peak from near Cottonwood Pass

as it passes through magnificent stands of ancient foxtail pine, vibrant meadows, and the wonderful alpine environment of the high Sierra. Deer and colorful wildflowers are plentiful along Rock Creek and in Crabtree Meadow. The dozens of luxuriant meadows are teeming with lush new growth, flowers, and wildlife, including an occasional bear.

TRAILHEAD FACILITIES

There are twelve walk-in campground sites, toilets, and piped water near the trailhead.

HOW TO GET THERE

From the signal light in Lone Pine on US 395, drive 3.5 miles west on the Whitney Portal Road. Turn south onto Horseshoe Meadow Road and continue 20.5 miles to Horseshoe Meadow and the Cottonwood Pass trailhead (not to be confused with the Cottonwood Lakes and New Army Pass trailhead). The paved road usually is open from May to late October.

BEAR-PROOF WILDERNESS FOOD STORAGE BOX LOCATIONS

▲ **Pacific Crest Trail and Lower Rock Creek Crossing:** One box is located about 5 feet southwest of the trail on the south side of the crossing.
▲ **Lower Crabtree Meadow and Pacific Crest Trail:** A box is located about 75 yards south of the Whitney Creek Crossing on the west side of the trail.
▲ **Crabtree Meadow:** One box has been placed southeast of the creek about 0.1 mile south of the Crabtree Patrol Cabin near the creek crossing.

ROUTE DESCRIPTION

Mile 0 to 3.5 (Horseshoe Meadow to Cottonwood Pass)
For the first 2 miles the Cottonwood Pass Trail skirts Horseshoe Meadow, gaining only 200 feet in the process. At the upper end of the

meadow, the trail begins its upward climb to Cottonwood Pass, gaining about 1000 feet in less than 2 miles. The trail passes through some beautiful high Sierra Nevada meadow terrain with widely spaced lodgepole, limber, and foxtail pine.

Mile 3.5 to 8.1 (Cottonwood Pass to Siberian Pass Trail)

At the four-way trail junction just beyond Cottonwood Pass, turn right onto the Pacific Crest Trail toward Rock Creek. Follow the Pacific Crest Trail in a west–northwest direction as it gently traverses the southwest slopes of Cirque Peak into Sequoia National Park and onto the Siberian Pass Trail. Chicken Spring Lake and its outlet creek are soon passed. There are numerous excellent places to camp near the lake. After you cross the outlet creek, there is a short climb of about 300 feet. The Pacific Crest Trail is nearly flat over this segment, with several ups and downs along the way. Although the trail is about 100 feet lower at the junction with the Siberian Pass Trail, there is a gain of about 500 feet over this trail segment.

Mile 8.1 to 14
(Siberian Pass Trail to Lower Rock Creek Crossing)

At the Siberian Pass Trail junction, stay on the Pacific Crest Trail by angling left toward Lower Rock Creek Crossing. The first 2 miles of this trail segment are nearly flat, with a few ups and downs. Over the last couple of miles the trail drops about 1000 feet to Rock Creek. As one drops into Rock Creek there are excellent views of Mount Langley, Joe Devel, Mount Pickering, Mount Chamberlin, Mount Mallory, and Mount LeConte to the north. At the trail junction near Rock Creek, turn left and hike along the creek, passing the ranger station on the way to Lower Rock Creek Crossing. There is a bear-proof wilderness food storage box on the south side of the creek crossing about 5 feet southwest of the trail.

Alternatively, instead of turning left toward Lower Rock Creek Crossing at the Siberian Pass Trail junction, you can leave the Pacific Crest Trail by turning right toward Rock Creek Trail and Lower Soldier Lake. This option is slightly longer but affords a worthwhile side trip to beautiful Lower Soldier Lake and passes through numerous lush alpine meadows along Rock Creek. Deer are often seen browsing in these meadows. This is also the trail segment that connects the Cottonwood Pass Trail with the New Army Pass Route.

Mile 14 to 16.8 (Lower Rock Creek Crossing to Guyot Pass)

Cross Rock Creek on a log and begin the ascent to Guyot Pass, a climb of 1360 feet over about 2.8 miles. The hike out of the Rock Creek canyon is steep for the first 600 feet. After this initial climb, the rate of ascent slackens. Near the 10,400-foot level, the trail crosses Guyot Creek. Many excellent campsites are nearby among the widely spaced foxtail pine. At Guyot Pass, one can climb the ridge, over easy terrain, to the summit of Mount Guyot with its 360-degree views of the Sierra Nevada and Mount Whitney.

Mile 16.8 to 20.4 (Guyot Pass to Lower Crabtree Meadow)

From the Guyot Pass, the Pacific Crest Trail skirts Guyot Flat and gradually descends to Lower Crabtree Meadow. Mount Whitney comes briefly into view for the first time about 0.5 mile before you cross Whitney Creek at Lower Crabtree Meadow. At Lower Crabtree Meadow there is a bear-proof food storage box located about 75 yards south of the Whitney Creek crossing on the west side of the Pacific Crest Trail.

Mile 20.4 to 24.2 (Lower Crabtree Meadow to Guitar Lake)

At the trail junction in Lower Crabtree Meadow, take the right fork leading to the Crabtree Patrol Cabin and Guitar Lake. From Lower Crabtree Meadow to the Crabtree Patrol Cabin it is about 1.3 miles with a slight climb of about 400 feet. A bear-proof food storage box has been placed southeast of the creek about 0.1 mile from the Crabtree Patrol Cabin near the creek crossing.

Before reaching the Crabtree Patrol Cabin, turn left and cross the creek. Join the John Muir Trail by tuning right toward Timberline Lake and Guitar Lake. From this trail junction it is about 1 mile to Timberline Lake. The area around Timberline Lake is closed to camping. From the lake, the John Muir Trail climbs about 500 feet to Guitar Lake. Consider camping near Guitar Lake or continue about 0.3 mile and camp near a tarn at 11,600 feet. There are also numerous campsites a little higher at the 11,900-foot level near a series of small tarns linked by a small stream flowing toward Hitchcock Lakes.

The stone hut on the summit of Mount Whitney was built in 1908.

Mile 24.2 to 27.7 (Guitar Lake to Mount Whitney Trail)

From Guitar Lake, the John Muir Trail climbs steadily for 3.5 miles and nearly 2000 feet up the steep west slopes of Whitney. A series of switchbacks seems endless but finally ends at the junction with the Mount Whitney Trail. The views of Hitchcock Lakes, Guitar Lake, and the mountain panorama steadily improve as you gain elevation. The trail itself is impressive as it climbs through the talus, large rock faces, and imposing granite towers. This segment of trail and the ninety-seven switchbacks below Trail Crest on the east side (Mount Whitney Trail, Route 6) are engineering marvels and tributes to the workers who built them. At the John Muir–Mount Whitney Trail junction there are several large tent platforms that can serve as campsites, but bring plenty of water because these campsites are dry.

Mile 27.7 to 29.7
(Mount Whitney Trail to Mount Whitney)

There are only 2 more miles to the summit and a little more than 1000 feet of elevation gain. The most difficult hiking is over as the trail gradually reaches the highest point in the Lower 48. Drop your pack and head for the summit. If you are not suffering from the altitude, the next 2 miles will be enjoyable as the trail snakes through impressive rock towers and past windows in the Sierra Nevada crest that provide breathtaking views of Trail Camp, the Mount Whitney

Trail, and the Owens Valley far below. On the other hand, this may be the most strenuous portion of the trip because the altitude may have depleted your strength, energy, and desire to continue.

The trail along the west side of the crest provides an excellent opportunity to scramble up Mount Muir and to bag the four 14,000-foot subpeaks of Mount Whitney: Aiguille Extra, Third Needle, Crooks Peak (also known as Day Needle), and Keeler Needle. Each of these peaks is only a couple hundred feet above the trail. From the junction of the Mount Whitney Trail, ascend the two switchbacks and proceed to a large rock cairn marking the cutoff to Mount Muir. The summit of Mount Muir is visible from this point on the trail. Ascend a shallow gully of loose scree and head toward the notch in the ridge to the right of the main summit. From this notch, angle left and scramble up a small chimney. Traverse left across a sloping ledge. Climb a crack to your right, gaining the small summit block. There is room for only three or four carefully placed climbers on the top at any one time. The top 50 feet of climbing is Class 3. From the summit there are impressive views of the east face of Mount Muir directly below, ninety-seven switchbacks in the Mount Whitney Trail, Trail Camp, Consultation Lake, Arc Pass, Whitney Portal, and the Owens Valley far below.

To ascend any of the four 14,000-foot subpeaks of Mount Whitney, leave the trail and scramble up the west slopes to the summit of these needles. All are easy Class 2 scrambling and provide a bird's-eye view of the sheer, nearly vertical east face. The top of each needle is visible from the trail. To reach the top of the first needle, Aiguille Extra, leave the trail about 1 mile from the trail junction and scramble to the top. The others follow in quick succession. For the last and highest needle, Keeler Needle, leave the trail before it turns west, heading away from the crest and the trail's final switchbacks.

From the summit of Whitney you will be greeted with impressive views of Mount Langley and Mount Muir to the south; the Kaweah Range and Sawtooth Peak to the west; Mount Russell, Tulainyo Lake (to the right of Mount Russell), the highest large alpine lake in the Sierra Nevada, Mount Williamson, Milestone Mountain, Table Mountain, and Thunder Mountain to the north; and Trail Camp, Mount Whitney Trail switchbacks, Consultation Lake, and Owens Valley to the east. If the weather is nice, spend some time on top; take in the scenery and savor your accomplishment.

After an hour on the summit it is time to consider the hike out. Return to your pack and hike out the Mount Whitney Trail. For a description of the trail, refer to Route 6.

Chapter 6

Westside Trailheads

The trails on the west side of the Sierra Nevada (Routes 10–13) originate in Sequoia and Kings Canyon National Parks. Sequoia National
Park became the second of our national parks shortly after the designation of Yosemite as a national park in 1890. Sequoia and Kings
Canyon National Parks are blessed with deep canyons, sheer granite
faces, glaciated lake basins, lush meadows, high peaks, and massive
giant sequoia trees. The Kings Canyon reaches a depth of 8200 feet
near the confluence of the middle and south forks of the Kings River.
The depth of this canyon is without peer in North America. It is deeper
than Hells Canyon in Idaho and the Grand Canyon in Arizona. At
Roads End, the start of the Bubbs Creek Trail (Route 10), one can stand
in the flat, glacial valley and peer up at the canyon walls rising nearly
a mile overhead. The Kern Canyon in Sequoia National Park (Routes
11–13) is 6000 feet deep, and several other prominent canyons, such
as the Middle Fork of the Kaweah River Canyon, exceed 4000 feet.

John Muir explored the many canyons of the Kings River and in
November 1891 penned an article for *The Century Illustrated Monthly
Magazine* titled "The Cañon of the South Fork of Kings River: A Rival
of the Yosemite," in which he wrote,

In the vast Sierra wilderness far to the southward of the famous Yosemite Valley, there is a yet grander valley of the same kind. It is situated on the south fork of Kings River, above the most extensive groves and forests of the giant sequoia, and beneath the shadows the highest mountains in the range, where the cañons are deepest and the snow-laden peaks are crowded most closely together. It is called the Big King's River Cañon, or King's River Yosemite. It is about ten miles long, half a mile wide, and the stupendous rocks of purplish gray granite that form the walls are from 2500 to 5000 feet in height, while the depth of the valley below the general surface of the mountain mass from which it has been carved is considerably more than a mile. Thus it appears that this new Yosemite is longer and deeper, and lies embedded in grander mountains, than the well-known Yosemite of the Merced. Their general characters, however are wonderfully alike, and they bear the same relationship to the fountains of the ancient glaciers above them.

Kings Canyon National Park is known for its deep canyons, whereas Sequoia National Park is known for its magnificent giant sequoia trees and high mountain summits. Giant sequoia trees, among the earth's largest living things, are commonly called Big Trees or Sierra redwoods but are distinctly different from the coastal redwoods of California. The giant sequoia has a columnlike trunk, huge stout branches, and cinnamon-colored bark. The taller and more slender coastal redwood is more coniferlike in shape. Route 11, the High Sierra Trail, starts in Crescent Meadow among the giant sequoia, not far from the world-famous Giant Forest.

John Muir explored the Sequoia and Kings Canyon area before they were designated as national parks and named the Giant Forest, where four of the world's five largest trees stand. His writings and descriptions of the canyons, giant sequoia groves, and lofty summits were partially responsible for the area being designated a national park. About the Giant Forest, John Muir observed in *Our National Parks,*

When I entered the sublime wilderness the day was nearly done, the trees with rosy, glowing countenances seemed to be hushed and thoughtful, as if waiting in conscious religious dependence on the sun, and one naturally walked softly and awe-stricken among them.

To the east of the deep canyons and the majestic groves of giant sequoia are magnificent mountains, meadows, glaciated cirques, and alpine lakes. This area is excellent for exploring, hiking, fishing, mountain climbing, ski mountaineering and simply enjoying the superb scenery. Officially, the Sequoia and Kings Canyon National Parks boundaries extend to the Sierra Nevada crest and include Mount Whitney and the other five 14,000-foot peaks described in this guidebook.

The four westside approaches to Mount Whitney (Routes 10–13) are rather long (43.2, 61.1, 49, and 59.3 miles, respectively). However, these trails pass through breathtaking terrain, making a rewarding and long-remembered wilderness experience. These trips require a 5- to 8-day commitment but are well worth it. After summiting, descend the Mount Whitney Trail and exit at Whitney Portal on the east side rather than retracing the long trail back to your starting point. This will save you many miles of hiking and several days in the wilderness but necessitates car shuttle arrangements (see Appendix 5 for the phone numbers of trailhead shuttle services).

Like the eastside trails, the westside trails also join the John Muir Trail at various points before ascending to the summit of Mount Whitney. The Bubbs Creek Trail (Route 10) joins the John Muir Trail at Vidette Meadows about 30 trail miles north of Mount Whitney. The High Sierra Trail (Route 11) and the Franklin Pass Trail (Route 12) intersect the John Muir Trail at Wallace Creek about 11 trail miles north of Whitney. The Farewell Gap Trail (Route 13) traverses to the south of Whitney and follows the John Muir Trail the last 9 miles.

When you request a wilderness permit, make sure that the National Park Service knows of your plans to climb Mount Whitney because your wilderness permit must include permission to enter the Mount Whitney Zone.

HOW TO GET THERE

Access to the four westside trails is via three main roads from the towns of Fresno, Visalia, and Three Rivers. Fresno is located on Highway 99 near the geographic center of the state. It is about 220 miles north of Los Angeles and 170 miles south of Sacramento. Visalia is slightly south of Fresno on Highway 198. Three Rivers is a small town about 40 miles east of Visalia on Highway 198. Highway 180 from Fresno, Highway 198 from Visalia, and the Mineral King Road from Three Rivers are the main roads to the westside trailheads. The following table summarizes these access roads to the various westside trailheads.

Westside Trailheads Route	Trailhead and Elevation	Access Road	Nearest Town	Town to Trailhead
10. Bubbs Creek Trail	Roads End, 5,035 feet	Highway 180	Squaw Valley and Fresno	40 miles from the park entrance
11. High Sierra Trail	Crescent Meadow, 6,700 feet	Highway 198 to Crescent Meadow Road	Three Rivers and Visalia	20 miles from the park entrance
12. Franklin Pass Trail	Mineral King, 7,800 feet	Highway 198 to Mineral King Road	Three Rivers and Visalia	25 miles from Highway 198
13. Farewell Gap Trail	Same as Route 12	Same as Route 12	Same as Route 12	Same as Route 12

ROUTE 10: BUBBS CREEK TRAIL

Trailhead ▲ Roads End, Kings Canyon National Park, 5035 feet

Rating ▲ Class 1

Distance ▲ 43.2 miles to the summit

Elevation gain ▲ 12,776 feet

Effort factor ▲ 34.4 hours

Trip duration ▲ 5–7 days

Maps ▲ The Sphinx, Mount Clarence King, Mount Brewer, Mount Williamson, and Mount Whitney (1:24,000); Marion Peak, Mount Pinchot, and Mount Whitney (1:62,500); or Tom Harrison Maps, Sequoia and Kings Canyon National Parks Map (1:125,000)

Trail Profile Table: Bubbs Creek Trail

Milepost	Elevation (feet)	Elevation/ Mileage Change	Trail Grade (feet/miles)
Roads End (0.0)	5,035	0.0/0.0	0.0
Bubbs Creek Trail (2.0)	5,098	63/2.0	32
Junction Meadow (10.5)	8,160	3,062/8.5	292
Vidette Meadows (13.4)	9,600	1,440/2.9	497
Forester Pass (21.4)	13,120	3,520/8.0	440
Shepherd Pass Trail (26.4)	11,000	-2,120/5.0	-424
Crabtree Patrol Cabin (35.2)	10,700	900/8.8	up/down
Guitar Lake (37.7)	11,500	800/2.5	320
Mount Whitney Trail (41.2)	13,480	1,980/3.5	566
Mount Whitney (43.2)	14,491	1,011/2.0	506

IN A NUTSHELL

This is the most direct and shortest of the westside trails. However, at only 5035 feet, this is the lowest starting point of any trail in this guidebook. Because of this low starting point, you will gain more than 12,000 feet in elevation over 43.2 miles. The beautiful Bubbs Creek Trail is a very popular hiking route into the Sierra Nevada

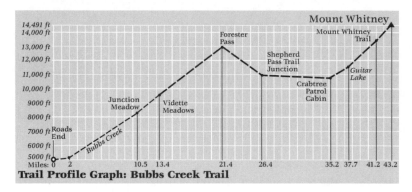

Trail Profile Graph: Bubbs Creek Trail

wilderness, so it is advisable to secure a wilderness permit through advance reservations.

The trail starts on the floor of Kings Canyon in beautiful Zumwalt Meadows. The sheer granite walls of the spectacular South Fork Kings River Canyon tower more than 5000 feet overhead. From Roads End, the sandy trail follows the South Fork Kings River for 2 miles, then ascends Bubbs Creek to Junction Meadow (Bubbs Creek) and continues to Vidette Meadows, where the route joins the John Muir Trail. From this point the route follows the trail described in Route 1 by ascending the beautiful glaciated valley to Forester Pass (the highest pass on the John Muir Trail), where the trail crosses the Kings–Kern Divide. Forester Pass is reached in 21.4 miles and 8000 feet in elevation gain. The good news is that at this point, two-thirds of the total amount of elevation to be gained along this route has been completed. From Forester Pass, the trail descends to the Shepherd Pass Trail junction and continues to Wallace Creek, Crabtree Meadow, and Guitar Lake and onto the summit.

TRAILHEAD FACILITIES

There is a National Park Service ranger station (no phone or electricity) at the Roads End trailhead, where wilderness permits can be picked up. At Cedar Grove (6 miles west of Roads End) there is a visitor center (phone 559-565-3793), store, market, restaurant, gift shop, books, maps, and bear-proof canisters. Four campgrounds are nearby: Sentinel (83 sites), Sheep Creek (111 sites), Canyon View (23 sites), and Moraine (120 sites).

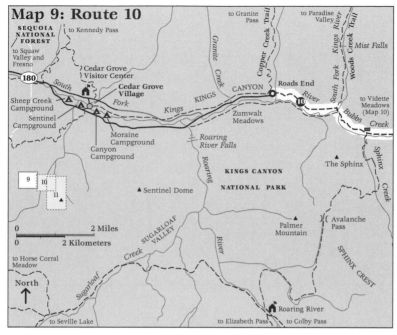

Map 9: Route 10

SEQUOIA
NATIONAL
FOREST
to Squaw
Valley and
Fresno

to Kennedy Pass

to Granite
Pass

Copper Creek Trail

to Paradise
Valley

Granite Creek

Kings River

South Fork

Woods Creek Trail

Mist Falls

Cedar Grove
Visitor Center

Cedar Grove
Village

180

South

Fork

Kings

KINGS

CANYON

Roads End

10

to Vidette
Meadows
(Map 10)

Sheep Creek
Campground

Sentinel
Campground

Moraine
Campground

Canyon
Campground

Zumwalt
Meadows

Bubbs

Creek

Roaring
River Falls

KINGS CANYON

Sphinx Creek

The Sphinx

9   10
   11

▲ Sentinel Dome

NATIONAL PARK

Roaring

River

0   2 Miles
0   2 Kilometers

to Horse Corral
Meadow

North
↑

Sugarloaf

Creek

SUGARLOAF
VALLEY

Palmer
Mountain

Avalanche
Pass

SPHINX CREST

to Seville Lake

to Elizabeth Pass

Roaring River

to Colby Pass

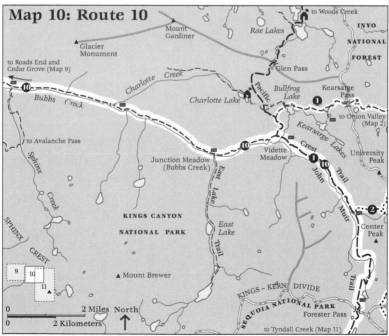

Map 10: Route 10

to Woods Creek

Mount
Gardiner

Rae Lakes

INYO

NATIONAL

FOREST

Glacier
Monument

to Roads End and
Cedar Grove (Map 9)

Charlotte   Creek

Glen Pass

Pacific

Bullfrog
Lake

Kearsarge
Pass

10

Bubbs   Creek

Charlotte Lake

1

to Onion Valley
(Map 2)

to Avalanche Pass

Sphinx Creek

Junction Meadow
(Bubbs Creek)

East Lake Trail

10

Vidette
Meadow

Kearsarge Lakes

Crest

John

1

10

University
Peak

SPHINX   CREST

KINGS CANYON

NATIONAL PARK

▲ Mount Brewer

East
Lake

Muir

2

Center
Peak

9   10
   11

0   2 Miles North
0   2 Kilometers   ↑

KINGS - KERN   DIVIDE

SEQUOIA NATIONAL PARK

Trail

Forester Pass

to Tyndall Creek (Map 11)

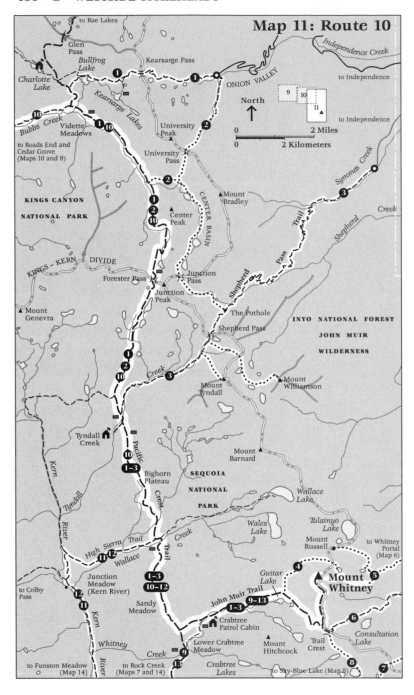

Map 11: Route 10

HOW TO GET THERE

From Fresno on Highway 99, drive east on Highway 180 (Kings Canyon Highway), into Kings Canyon National Park. Cedar Grove and Roads End are 34 and 40 miles, respectively, from the park entrance. The road to Cedar Grove and Roads End is closed in the winter after the first major snowfall and usually is opened in the spring by the end of April. Call the National Park Service or Caltrans for road conditions (see Appendix 5).

BEAR-PROOF WILDERNESS FOOD STORAGE BOX LOCATIONS

▲ **Sphinx Creek (2 boxes):** One box is located above the Bubbs Creek Trail east of the crossing; a second box is located across the creek on the Avalanche Pass Trail (Sphinx Creek Trail).

▲ **Charlotte Creek:** One box has been placed below the Bubbs Creek Trail east of the crossing.

▲ *Junction Meadow (Lower):* A box is located next to the trail below Junction Meadow.

▲ **Junction Meadow (East Creek):** This box is located on the west side of the East Lake Trail just south of the log crossing Bubbs Creek.

▲ **Vidette Meadows (2 boxes):** One box is located at Lower Vidette Meadow about 0.1 mile west of the John Muir Trail junction on the south side of the Bubbs Creek Trail; the second box at East Vidette is located about 0.2 mile on the John Muir Trail above the Bubbs Creek–John Muir Trail junction on the south side of the trail.

▲ **John Muir Trail and Center Basin Trail:** A box has been placed below the trail approximately 150 yards south of the trail junction (0.25 mile north of the Center Basin Creek crossing).

▲ **Wheelbarrow Camp:** One box is located in the first group of trees north of Forester Pass.

▲ **John Muir Trail and Tyndall Creek Crossing:** One box is located west of the trail about 350 feet north of the creek.

▲ **Tyndall Creek Frog Ponds:** A box is located about 0.5 mile south of Tyndall Creek Crossing on the east side of the trail.

▲ **John Muir Trail and Wallace Creek Crossing:** One box has been placed west of the trail about 100 feet south of the creek crossing.

▲ **Crabtree Meadow:** A box is located about 100 yards southeast of the John Muir Trail and about 100 yards south of the Crabtree Patrol Cabin.

ROUTE DESCRIPTION

Mile 0 to 2 (Roads End to Bubbs Creek Trail)

The sandy trail along the South Fork Kings River is nearly flat, gaining only 63 feet in 2 miles. Many large pine, cedar, and oak trees grow on the broad valley floor. As you hike along the river, the sheer granite walls of the canyon tower overhead. Your neck may become stiff from constantly straining to see the towering and inspiring rock faces. The South Fork is an exceedingly powerful river during the spring and summer, when it is filled with icy snow runoff. The cascading falls along the river are impressive sights, drawing many sightseers. Because of its low elevation, the start of this trail can be hot even in the fall.

Mile 2 to 10.5 (Bubbs Creek to Junction Meadow)

At the junction of the Bubbs Creek Trail turn right and ascend the Bubbs Creek Trail. The trail climbs steeply for 1 mile, gaining about 1000 feet. After this initial climb, the trail continues its upstream ascent but at a more leisurely rate. The views of Bubbs Creek and Sphinx Creek, as they cascade down the steep canyon walls, are spectacular. This is especially true in spring and early summer, when these creeks are roaring with snowmelt from the high mountains above. The trail soon passes the Avalanche Pass Trail (Sphinx Creek Trail) junction after 2.1 miles. Just beyond this trail junction, on the left side of the trail, are numerous excellent campsites with a bear-proof food storage box and a pit toilet. Continue east on the Bubbs Creek Trail to Junction Meadow. Along this popular trail the National Park Service has placed bear-proof food storage boxes at Sphinx Creek, Charlotte Creek, lower Junction Meadow, and East Creek in Junction Meadow. If time permits, a side trip to East Lake is worth the effort.

Mile 10.5 to 13.4 (Junction Meadow to Vidette Meadows)

Above Junction Meadow the Bubbs Creek Trail steepens as it climbs to Vidette Meadows. In the first mile the trail gains about 1000 feet and then levels off slightly for the rest of the way to the meadows. At Vidette Meadows the Bubbs Creek Trail meets the John Muir Trail.

Head south, on the John Muir Trail, toward Forester Pass. The route, from here on follows that of Route 1. There are several bear-proof food storage boxes in Vidette Meadows.

Mile 13.4 to 21.4 (Vidette Meadows to Forester Pass)
Refer to Route 1 for a description of this segment of trail.

Mile 21.4 to 26.4 (Forester Pass to Shepherd Pass Trail)
Refer to Route 1 for a description of this segment of trail.

Mile 26.4 to 35.2
(Shepherd Pass Trail to Crabtree Patrol Cabin)
Refer to Route 1 for a description of this segment of trail.

Mile 35.2 to 37.7 (Crabtree Patrol Cabin to Guitar Lake)
Refer to Route 1 for a description of this segment of trail.

Mile 37.7 to 41.2 (Guitar Lake to Mount Whitney Trail)
Refer to Route 1 for a description of this segment of trail.

Mile 41.2 to 43.2
(Mount Whitney Trail to Mount Whitney)
Refer to Route 1 for a description of this segment of trail. After summiting, return to your pack and hike out the Mount Whitney Trail. For a description of the trail, refer to Route 6.

ROUTE 11: HIGH SIERRA TRAIL

Trailhead ▲ Crescent Meadow, Sequoia National Park, 6700 feet
Rating ▲ Class 1
Distance ▲ 61.1 miles to the summit
Elevation gain ▲ 14,851 feet
Effort factor ▲ 45.5 hours
Trip duration ▲ 6–8 days
Maps ▲ Giant Forest, Lodgepole, Triple Divide Peak, Mount Kaweah, Chagoopa Falls, and Mount Whitney (1:24,000); Triple Divide Peak, Kern Peak, and Mount Whitney (1:62,500); or Tom Harrison Maps, Mount Whitney High Country Map (1:63,360)

Trail Profile Table: High Sierra Trail

Milepost	Elevation (feet)	Elevation/ Mileage Change	Trail Grade (feet/miles)
Crescent Meadow (0.0)	6,700	0.0/0.0	0.0
Bearpaw Meadow (11.3)	7,840	1,900/11.3	up/down
Kaweah Gap (19.9)	10,660	3,860/8.6	up/down
Big Arroyo Trail (22.5)	9,600	-1,060/2.6	-408
Upper Funston Meadow (34.5)	6,800	1,000/-3,800/12.0	up/down
Junction Meadow (44.2)	8,000	1,200/9.7	124
John Muir Trail at Wallace Creek (48.9)	10,400	2,400/4.7	511
Crabtree Patrol Cabin (53.1)	10,700	700/4.2	up/down
Guitar Lake (55.6)	11,500	800/2.5	320
Mount Whitney Trail (59.1)	13,480	1,980/3.5	566
Mount Whitney (61.1)	14,491	1,011/2.0	506

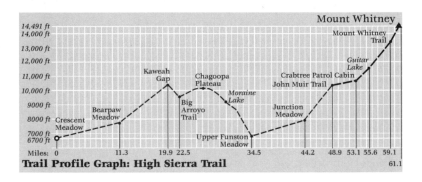

Trail Profile Graph: High Sierra Trail

IN A NUTSHELL

The High Sierra Trail starts at Crescent Meadow among the giant sequoia trees of Sequoia National Park. The trail climbs high above the Middle Fork of the Kaweah River, past the High Sierra summer camp at Bearpaw Meadow, under the impressive face of the Angel Wings,

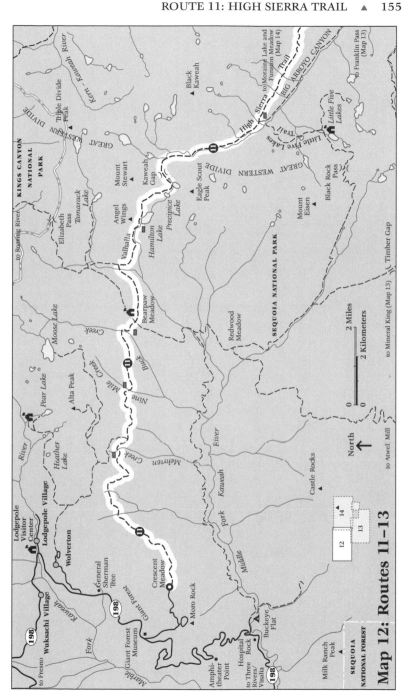

Map 12: Routes 11–13

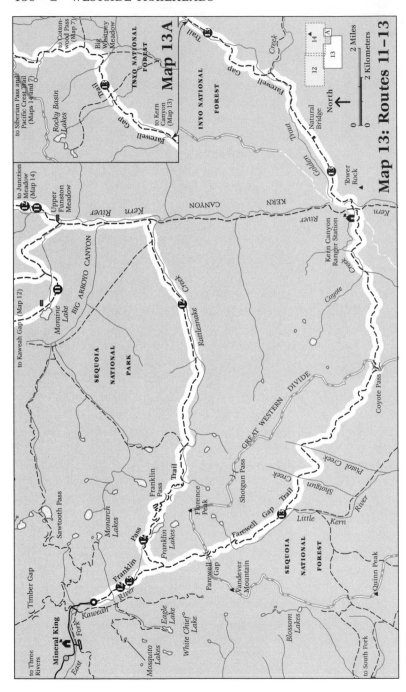

Map 13: Routes 11–13

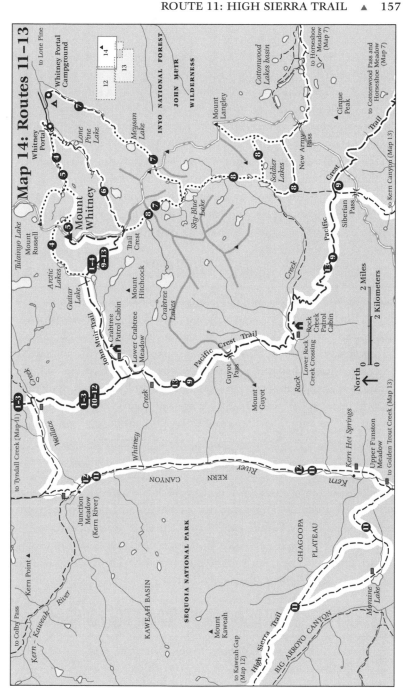

Map 14: Routes 11–13

through the Valhalla, past beautiful Hamilton Lake, and up to Precipice Lake. Precipice Lake is the location of a famous Ansel Adams photograph. The scenery and terrain are exceptional along this trail. Beyond Precipice Lake, the High Sierra Trail crosses the Great Western Divide at Kaweah Gap, passes by Nine Lakes Basin, crosses the Chagoopa Plateau, and drops into the Kern Canyon at Upper Funston Meadow. Here the trail turns north up the Kern River, past the Kern Hot Springs to Junction Meadow (Kern River) to Wallace Creek, joining the John Muir Trail at this point. The remainder of the route follows the John Muir Trail and Route 1 to the summit of Whitney.

The High Sierra Trail and Routes 4 and 8 are my favorites. The scenery along the High Sierra Trail rivals that of any found in Yosemite.

TRAILHEAD FACILITIES

The Lodgepole Visitor Center (phone 559-565-3782) is several miles beyond the turnoff to Crescent Meadow and the High Sierra trailhead. Pick up your wilderness permits next to the visitor center at the ranger station (phone 559-565-3775). Many services are nearby, including the Giant Forest Museum, a nature center, Crystal Cave, horseback riding, food, shops, market, deli, gift shop, snack bar, showers, laundry, and bear-proof canisters. There are also picnic areas and campgrounds: Lodgepole (204 sites) and Dorst (201 sites).

HOW TO GET THERE

From Fresno, drive south on Highway 99 for 36 miles and turn east on Highway 198 to Visalia. Continue east to the town of Three Rivers and into Sequoia National Park. From the park entrance, drive 17 miles over a twisting road to the Giant Forest and Museum. Turn right to Moro Rock and the High Sierra Trailhead at Crescent Meadow. The trailhead is at the end of Crescent Meadow Road.

BEAR-PROOF WILDERNESS FOOD STORAGE BOX LOCATIONS

▲ **High Sierra Trail and Mehrten Creek Crossing:** A box is situated about 40 feet above the trail on the west side of the creek.
▲ **High Sierra Trail and Nine Mile Creek Crossing:** One box is located by the trail on the west side of the creek.

Angel Wings from Hamilton Lake on the High Sierra Trail (Route 11)

▲ **High Sierra Trail and Buck Creek Crossing:** A box is located at camp on the west side of the creek.

▲ **Bearpaw Meadow:** Four boxes are located in the main camp area.

▲ **Upper Hamilton Lake:** One box is located in the open rocky area on the west side of the lake; a second box is 200 yards west of the lake on the south side of the outlet stream.

▲ **Big Arroyo Crossing and Patrol Cabin:** A box is located on the east side of Big Arroyo Creek about 100 feet southeast of the Kaweah Gap–Little Five Lakes–Big Arroyo Creek trail junction.

▲ **Moraine Lake:** One box is adjacent to the trail along the east shore of the lake.

▲ **Upper Funston Meadow:** One box is located southeast of the hitching rail at the northeast corner of the meadow near the river; the second box is located near a campsite 60 yards farther south.

▲ **Kern Hot Springs:** One box is located between the trail and the river; the second one is 50 yards east of the trail in an open stand of Jeffrey pine.

▲ **Junction Meadow (Kern River):** One box is located next to the High Sierra Trail near the southeast corner of Junction Meadow, 230 yards north of the Wallace Creek stream crossing and 200 yards south of the junction with the Colby Pass Trail.

▲ **John Muir Trail and Wallace Creek Crossing:** One box has been placed west of the trail about 100 feet south of the creek crossing.

▲ **Crabtree Meadow:** One box is located southeast of the creek and about 0.1 mile south of the Crabtree Patrol Cabin near the creek crossing.

ROUTE DESCRIPTION

Mile 0 to 11.3 (Crescent Meadow to Bearpaw Meadow)

The trail soon leaves Crescent Meadow and the giant sequoia trees and begins the long traverse of the steep south-facing slopes high above the Middle Fork Kaweah River. Because of this southerly exposure, the trail can be hot even in late October. An early morning start is suggested to beat the heat. Although there are numerous ups and downs along this segment of trail, the High Sierra Trail gradually gains elevation from the 6700-foot Crescent Meadow trailhead to 7840 feet at

Bearpaw Meadow. The High Sierra Trail crosses Mehrten Creek (7640 feet) at milepost 5.8. At this creek crossing there are three campsites, a fire pit, and a bear-proof food storage box. There is another bear-proof food storage locker at the Nine Mile Creek trail crossing. And just before making the final 400-foot climb to Bearpaw Meadow, the trail crosses Buck Creek. There is a bear-proof food storage box at this crossing as well. The High Sierra Camp and Ranger Station are located at Bearpaw Meadow. The designated camping area for back-packers is just before and below Bearpaw Meadow. There are four bear-proof food storage boxes in the main camp area.

Mile 11.3 to 19.9 (Bearpaw Meadow to Kaweah Gap)

The scenery along this trail segment changes dramatically. From the trailhead to Bearpaw Meadow, the trail traverses country that is heavily timbered with evergreens, offering limited vistas of the mountains and glaciated domes ahead. Beyond Bearpaw Meadow, the trees and vistas open up, and the terrain becomes more alpine. At Lone Pine Creek the trail crosses a deep gorge on a spectacular 50-foot-long bridge. Beyond the bridge, the trail traverses beneath the impressive granite face of the Angel Wings, continues through the Valhalla, ascends a series of switchbacks to Hamilton Lake, and passes through a tunnel on its way to Precipice Lake and Kaweah Gap. In places the trail is perched on the top of sheer granite faces with overhanging cliffs.

In the first 1.6 miles after leaving Bearpaw Meadow, the trail loses elevation slightly, crosses the spectacular gorge of Lone Pine Creek, and passes the Elizabeth Pass Trail junction (7500 feet). In another 2.4 miles the trail passes upper Hamilton Lake. On its way to Hamilton Lake, the trail gains and then loses about 400 feet of elevation as it passes below the sheer granite face of the Angel Wings.

The camping and scenery at Hamilton Lake is second to none. The sights along this trail segment and at Hamilton Lake are as spectacular as any found in Yosemite Valley. It is difficult to imagine a camping environment superior to that of this area. Hamilton Lake is situated in a magnificent amphitheater surrounded by the sheer granite walls of Eagle Scout Peak, Mount Stewart, and the Angel Wings. While camping under the stars one can fall asleep viewing the awesome moonlit face of the Angel Wings and in the morning wake up to the red glow of the sunrise on its sheer granite face. Not to be outdone by the sleeping area, the pit toilet provides unmatched views as well. Two bear-proof storage boxes have been placed near the lake.

From Hamilton Lake (8235 feet), climb 2000 feet over 4 miles to Precipice Lake (10,300 feet) and continue another 0.6 mile to Kaweah Gap (10,660 feet).

Mile 19.9 to 22.5 (Kaweah Gap to Big Arroyo Trail)

From Kaweah Gap you will have excellent views of Triple Divide Peak, Black Kaweah, the Kaweah Peaks, and Nine Lakes Basin. Black Kaweah is one of the great mountain summits of the Sierra Nevada. Because of its remoteness and climbing difficulty, the peak is seldom climbed. From Kaweah Gap, the trail descends about 1000 feet in 2.6 miles over gentle terrain. The High Sierra Trail follows the Big Arroyo to a three-way junction: the Big Arroyo Trail, the Little Five Lakes/Black Rock Pass Trail, and the High Sierra Trail. A bear-proof food storage box is located near this trail junction. At this three-way intersection, take the left fork (the High Sierra Trail) toward the Chagoopa Plateau.

Mile 22.5 to 34.5
(Big Arroyo Trail to Upper Funston Meadow)

From this three-way junction, the High Sierra Trail gradually gains about 1000 feet over the next 3.5 miles to 10,600 feet. The trail then starts a gradual descent, and in 1.5 miles the trail junction to Moraine Lake is reached. The more direct route is to take the left fork and bypass Moraine Lake. However, taking the trail to beautiful Moraine Lake adds only 0.8 mile of hiking. There is a bear-proof food storage box at Moraine Lake. The High Sierra Trail (left fork) crosses Chagoopa Creek twice before reaching Sky Parlor Meadow in 3.3 miles (from the trail junction). At Sky Parlor Meadow take the left fork and descend steeply to the Kern River and the Upper Funston Meadow. In 3.7 miles the trail drops 2400 feet, with most of the elevation loss coming in the last 2 miles just before Upper Funston Meadow. There are two bear-proof boxes at Upper Funston Meadow. Additionally, there is a pit toilet in the forest north of the meadow. An informal access trail leading to the Upper Funston Meadow campsites leaves the High Sierra Trail about 160 yards north of the meadow.

Black Kaweah, one of the great peaks of the Sierra Nevada. Because of its remoteness, the peak is seldom climbed.

Mile 34.5 to 44.2
(Upper Funston Meadow to Junction Meadow)

You are now in the heart of the Sierra Nevada and, surprisingly, your elevation is no greater than that of Crescent Meadow, your starting point 34 miles back. At the Upper Funston Meadow the trail heads north up the Kern River to Junction Meadow (Kern River). In the first mile the Chagoopa Falls is passed and in another 0.5 mile Kern Hot Springs is reached. This is a favorite of many tired backpackers. Two bear-proof food storage boxes are located near the hot springs, and a pit toilet is located behind a clump of manzanita near the bear-proof box. From Upper Funston Meadow to Junction Meadow (Kern River), the High Sierra Trail gains only 1200 feet over 9.7 miles. To add a bit of confusion, there are two Junction Meadows in the Sierra Nevada, and they are not far apart. Route 10 passes through Junction Meadow (Bubbs Creek) and is located about 12 miles due north of Junction Meadow (Kern River). At Junction Meadow (Kern River), there is a bear-proof box near the southeast corner of the meadow near Wallace Creek and the trail junction to Colby Pass.

Mile 44.2 to 48.9
(Junction Meadow to John Muir Trail at Wallace Creek)

At Junction Meadow (Kern River) the trail forks. The left fork heads to Colby Pass to the west and north, and the right fork continues north.

Take the right fork (High Sierra Trail) and continue up the Kern River for 1.3 miles. The trail steepens, gaining 800 feet over this segment. At the next trail junction, take the right fork that leaves the Kern River and ascends Wallace Creek to the John Muir Trail. Over the next 3.4 miles the trail gains elevation, rapidly ascending from 8800 feet to 10,400 feet. Upon joining the John Muir Trail, turn south (right) and follow the John Muir Trail and Route 1 to the summit of Whitney.

Mile 48.9 to 53.1
(Wallace Creek to Crabtree Meadow Patrol Cabin)
Refer to Route 1 for a description of this segment of trail.

Mile 53.1 to 55.6
(Crabtree Meadow Patrol Cabin to Guitar Lake)
Refer to Route 1 for a description of this segment of trail.

Mile 55.6 to 59.1 (Guitar Lake to Mount Whitney Trail)
Refer to Route 1 for a description of this segment of trail.

Mile 59.1 to 61.1 (Mount Whitney Trail to Mount Whitney)
Refer to Route 1 for a description of this segment of trail. After summiting, return to your pack at the junction of the John Muir Trail and the Mount Whitney Trail and hike out the Mount Whitney Trail. For a description of the trail, refer to Route 6.

Route 12: FRANKLIN PASS TRAIL

Trailhead ▲ Mineral King, Sequoia National Park, 7800 feet
Rating ▲ Class 1
Distance ▲ 49 miles to the summit
Elevation gain ▲ 12,371 feet
Effort factor ▲ 36.9 hours
Trip duration ▲ 5–7 days
Maps ▲ Mineral King, Chagoopa Falls, Mount Kaweah, and Mount Whitney (1:24,000); Mineral King and Mount Whitney (1:62,500); or Tom Harrison Maps, Mount Whitney High Country (1:63,360)

Trail Profile Table: Franklin Pass Trail

Milepost	Elevation (feet)	Elevation/ Mileage Change	Trail Grade (feet/miles)
Mineral King (0.0)	7,800	0.0/0.0	0.0
Franklin Pass (8.4)	11,840	4,040/8.4	481
Kern River Trail (19.7)	6,560	-3,680/11.3	-404
Upper Funston Meadow (22.4)	6,800	240/2.7	89
Junction Meadow (32.1)	8,000	1,200/9.7	124
John Muir Trail at Wallace Creek (36.8)	10,400	2,400/4.7	511
Crabtree Patrol Cabin (41.0)	10,700	700/4.2	up/down
Guitar Lake (43.5)	11,500	800/2.5	320
Mount Whitney Trail (47.0)	13,480	1,980/3.5	566
Mount Whitney (49.0)	14,491	1,011/2.0	506

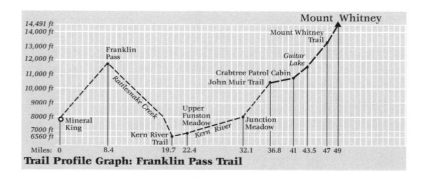

Trail Profile Graph: Franklin Pass Trail

IN A NUTSHELL

In the 1870s, miners flooded into Mineral King Valley on the wave of a silver rush. Several mines, including the Empire, White Chief, and Lady Franklin, were partially developed. However, by the end of the 1880s the silver rush and mining activity faded. One of the obvious results of the mining was the Mineral King road, which was completed in August 1879. Someone has painstakingly counted the 698 curves in the 25-mile long road. That's 28 curves per mile.

In the 1960s and 1970s, the Walt Disney Corporation attempted to construct a large alpine ski resort in the Mineral King Valley. A long and complicated legal battle followed. Finally on November 10, 1978, Congress transferred the management of the area from the Forest Service to the Sequoia National Park, ending any possibilities of massive development.

The Mineral King Valley is a unique and wonderful part of Sequoia National Park. In the summer, wildlife and flowers are abundant. The wildlife is very evident: deer, mountain lion, coyote, pine martens, wolverine, black bear, marmot, gray fox, bobcat, and trout in the lakes and streams. High alpine lakes, meadows, streams, and waterfalls abound. Numerous peaks and high passes ring the valley, providing countless hiking, camping, and fishing opportunities.

This route starts at Mineral King, an isolated and exceptionally beautiful portion of Sequoia National Park, and heads south up the Franklin Pass–Farewell Gap Trail. The trail passes through the impressive Franklin Lakes basin and climbs steeply over Franklin Pass and down the Rattlesnake Creek Trail to the Kern River. Here the route turns north up the Kern River, joining the High Sierra Trail at Upper Funston Meadow. At the Upper Funston Meadow, the route follows the High Sierra Trail (Route 11) to Junction Meadow (Kern River) and on to the John Muir Trail at Wallace Creek. From here, follow Route 1 by continuing south along the John Muir Trail to the summit of Whitney.

TRAILHEAD FACILITIES

The Mineral King Ranger Station (phone 559-565-3768) is located near the trailhead. There are two campgrounds (no trailers and RVs) in Mineral King Valley: Atwell Mill (21 sites) and Cold Springs (40 sites). Silver City Resort (privately owned), located about 7 miles from the trailhead, includes a store, restaurant, and lodging (phone 559-561-3223).

HOW TO GET THERE

To reach the Mineral King area of Sequoia National Park, drive 36 miles south of Fresno on Highway 99 to Highway 198. Turn east on Highway 198 to Visalia and proceed through the town of Three Rivers.

Beyond Three Rivers and about 2 miles before the entrance to Sequoia National Park, turn right onto the Mineral King Road, a long, narrow, winding road to Silver City and Mineral King Valley. Allow at least 90 minutes to drive the 25 miles to the trailhead.

The abundant wildlife in the area includes many marmots. Marmots have been known to damage cars by climbing into the engine compartment and eating hoses and wires. If parking your car for any length of time, consider placing chicken wire or a mesh completely around the car to keep the marmots out. Check with the park ranger for suggestions.

The north face of Sawtooth Peak in the Mineral King area (Route 12)
Photo by Guy McClure

BEAR-PROOF WILDERNESS FOOD STORAGE BOX LOCATIONS

▲ **Franklin Lakes (3 boxes):** One box is located below and east of the dam about 100 feet west of the trail, a second box has been placed about 0.25 mile east of the dam and southwest of the trail (take the trail at the pit toilet sign), and a third box is 0.4 mile east of the dam about 200 feet above the lake shore.

▲ **Upper Funston Meadow:** One box is located southeast of the hitchrail at the northeast corner of the meadow near the river; the second box is located near a campsite 60 yards farther south.

▲ **Kern Hot Springs:** One box is located between the trail and the river; the second one is 50 yards east of the trail in an open stand of Jeffrey pine.

▲ **Junction Meadow (Kern River):** A box is located next to the High Sierra Trail near the southeast corner of Junction Meadow, 230 yards north of the Wallace Creek stream crossing and 200 yards south of the junction with the Colby Pass Trail.

▲ **John Muir Trail and Wallace Creek Crossing:** One box has been placed west of the trail about 100 feet south of the creek crossing.

▲ **Pacific Crest Trail and Lower Crabtree Meadow:** One box is located about 75 yards south of the Whitney Creek Crossing on the west side of the trail.

▲ **Crabtree Meadow:** A box is located southeast of the creek about 0.1 mile south of the Crabtree Patrol Cabin near the creek crossing.

ROUTE DESCRIPTION

Mile 0 to 8.4 (Mineral King to Franklin Pass)

The Franklin Pass–Farewell Gap Trail heads south from the end of the road at Mineral King. Over the first 2 miles the gentle trail follows the East Fork Kaweah River as it ascends Farewell Canyon. Wildlife and wildflowers are abundant in this lush valley. Florence Peak, Vandever Mountain, White Chief Mountain, and many other impressive summits ring the canyon. After 2 miles, the trail steepens and over the next mile ascends several switchbacks to the junction of the Farewell Gap Trail (Route 13) and the Franklin Pass Trail (Route 12). Turn left up the Franklin Pass Trail as it leaves the valley floor and ascends to the Franklin Lakes basin and on to Franklin Pass. The Franklin Lakes basin is impressive as the north face of Florence Peak (the highest summit in the Mineral King area) looms directly above the lake. Three bear-proof food storage boxes have been placed at Franklin Lakes. Above Franklin Lakes a series of switchbacks ascends the steep west slopes of Franklin Pass.

Mile 8.4 to 19.7 (Franklin Pass to Kern River Trail)

From Franklin Pass (11,840 feet), the trail descends a series of switchbacks as the trail drops 1800 feet in the first couple of miles. Pass the Soda Creek Trail on the left and continue down along the Rattlesnake Creek Trail. The trail follows Rattlesnake Creek all the way to the Kern River. As the Kern River is approached, the trail steepens. All the elevation gained ascending Franklin Pass has now been lost as you drop to the 6560-foot level of Kern River Canyon.

Mile 19.7 to 22.4
(Kern River Trail to Upper Funston Meadow)

You are now in the heart of the Sierra Nevada and, surprisingly, your elevation is 1200 feet lower than your starting point at Mineral King. Turn north (left) and follow the nearly flat Kern River Trail north to Upper Funston Meadow. At Upper Funston Meadow the route joins the High Sierra Trail and Route 11 the rest of the way.

The John Muir Trail joins the Mount Whitney Trail about 2 miles from the summit of Mount Whitney.

Mile 22.4 to 32.1
(Upper Funston Meadow to Junction Meadow)

At Upper Funston Meadow the trail heads north up the Kern River to Junction Meadow (Kern River). In the first mile the Chagoopa Falls is passed and in another 0.5 mile Kern Hot Springs is reached. This is a favorite of many tired backpackers. Two bear-proof food storage boxes are located near the hot springs, and a pit toilet is located behind a clump of manzanita near the bear-proof box. From Upper Funston Meadow to Junction Meadow (Kern River), the High Sierra Trail gains only 1200 feet over 9.7 miles. To add confusion, there are two Junction Meadows in the Sierra Nevada and they are not far apart. Junction Meadow (Bubbs Creek, Route 10) is about 12 miles due north of Junction Meadow (Kern River). At Junction Meadow (Kern River), there is a bear-proof box near the southeast corner of the meadow near Wallace Creek and the trail junction to Colby Pass.

Mile 32.1 to 36.8
(Junction Meadow to John Muir Trail at Wallace Creek)

At Junction Meadow (Kern River) the trail forks. The left fork heads to Colby Pass to the west and north, and the right fork continues north. Take the right fork (High Sierra Trail) and continue up the Kern River for 1.3 miles. The trail steepens, gaining 800 feet over this segment. At the next trail junction, take the right fork that leaves the Kern River and ascends Wallace Creek to the John Muir Trail. Over the next 3.4 miles the trail gains elevation, rapidly ascending from 8800 feet to 10,400 feet. Upon joining the John Muir Trail, turn south (right) and follow the John Muir Trail and Route 1 to the summit of Mount Whitney.

Mile 36.8 to 41
(John Muir Trail at Wallace Creek to Crabtree Patrol Cabin)

Refer to Route 1 for a description of this segment of trail.

Mile 41 to 43.5 (Crabtree Patrol Cabin to Guitar Lake)

Refer to Route 1 for a description of this segment of trail.

Mile 43.5 to 47 (Guitar Lake to Mount Whitney Trail)

Refer to Route 1 for a description of this segment of trail.

Mile 47 to 49
(Mount Whitney Trail to Mount Whitney summit)

Refer to Route 1 for a description of this segment of trail. After summiting, return to your pack at the junction of the John Muir Trail and the Mount Whitney Trail and descend the Mount Whitney Trail. For a description of the trail, refer to Route 6.

Route 13: FAREWELL GAP TRAIL

Trailhead ▲ Mineral King, Sequoia National Park, 7800 feet

Rating ▲ Class 1

Distance ▲ 59.3 miles to the summit

Elevation gain ▲ 14,848 feet

Effort factor ▲ 44.6 hours

Trip duration ▲ 6–8 days

Maps ▲ Mineral King, Quinn Peak, Kern Lake, Kern Peak, Johnson Peak, and Mount Whitney (1:24,000); or Mineral King, Kern Peak, and Mount Whitney (1:62,500)

Trail Profile Table: Farewell Gap Trail

Milepost	Elevation (feet)	Elevation/ Mileage Change	Trail Grade (feet/miles)
Mineral King (0.0)	7,800	0.0/0.0	0.0
Farewell Gap (5.7)	10,587	2,787/5.7	489
Coyote Pass (14.7)	10,080	1,900/-2,407/9.0	up/down
Kern Canyon (20.6)	6,320	-3,760/5.9	-637
Siberian Pass (37.1)	10,960	4,640/16.5	281
Lower Rock Creek crossing (43.6)	9,520	-1,440/6.5	-222
Guyot Pass (46.4)	10,880	1,360/2.8	486
Lower Crabtree Meadow (50.0)	10,330	-550/3.6	-153
Guitar Lake (53.8)	11,500	1,170/3.8	308
Mount Whitney Trail (57.3)	13,480	1,980/3.5	566
Mount Whitney (59.3)	14,491	1,011/2.0	506

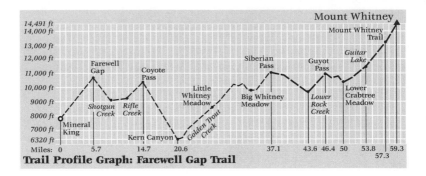

Trail Profile Graph: Farewell Gap Trail

IN A NUTSHELL

This is the most southerly route included in this guidebook and loops to the south of Sequoia National Park by initially heading south, then east and then north on its way to the summit of Whitney. The Farewell Gap Trail starts in Sequoia National Park at Mineral King and heads south over Farewell Gap, where it leaves Sequoia National Park. Here the trail turns southeast as it descends the Little Kern River to Shotgun Creek and Pistol Creek, where it then regains the lost elevation by ascending Coyote Pass. From this pass, the trail turns east and descends Coyote Creek to the Kern River and the Kern Canyon Ranger Station. Over the next 16.5 miles the trail gains 4600 feet, passing the Natural Bridge, Little Whitney Meadow, and Big Whitney Meadow on its way to Siberian Pass. The trail reenters Sequoia National Park at Siberian Pass, drops into Rock Creek following the Pacific Crest Trail north to Crabtree Meadow, where it joins the John Muir Trail to the summit of Mount Whitney. The trail traverses four passes (Farewell Gap, Coyote Pass, Siberian Pass, and Guyot Pass) as it gains 14,848 feet over 59.3 miles.

TRAILHEAD FACILITIES

The Mineral King Ranger Station (phone 559-565-3768) is located near the trailhead. Two campgrounds (no trailers and RVs) are located in Mineral King Valley: Atwell Mill (21 sites) and Cold Springs (40 sites). Silver City Resort (privately owned), located about 7 miles from the trailhead, includes a store, restaurant, and lodging (phone 559-561-3223).

HOW TO GET THERE

To reach the Mineral King area of Sequoia National Park, drive 36 miles south of Fresno on Highway 99 to Highway 198. Turn east on Highway 198 to Visalia and proceed through the town of Three Rivers. Beyond Three Rivers and about 2 miles before the entrance to Sequoia National Park, turn right onto Mineral King Road, a long, narrow, winding road to Silver City and Mineral King Valley. Allow at least 90 minutes to drive the 25 miles to the trailhead.

The area is rich in wildlife, including many marmots. Marmots have been known to damage cars by climbing into the engine compartment and eating hoses and wires. If parking your car for any length of time, consider placing chicken wire completely around your car to keep them out. Check with the park ranger for suggestions.

BEAR-PROOF WILDERNESS FOOD STORAGE BOX LOCATIONS

▲ **Pacific Crest Trail and Lower Rock Creek Crossing:** One box is located about 5 feet southwest of the trail on the south side of the crossing.

▲ **Lower Crabtree Meadow and Pacific Crest Trail:** A box is located about 75 yards south of the Whitney Creek Crossing on the west side of the trail.

▲ **Crabtree Meadow:** One box is located southeast of the creek about 0.1 mile south of the Crabtree Patrol Cabin near the creek crossing.

ROUTE DESCRIPTION

Mile 0 to 5.7 (Mineral King to Farewell Gap)

The Franklin Pass and Farewell Gap Trail heads south from the end of the road at Mineral King. Over the first 2 miles the gentle trail follows the East Fork Kaweah River as it ascends Farewell Canyon. Wildlife and wildflowers are abundant in this lush valley. Florence Peak, Vandever Mountain, White Chief Mountain, and many other impressive summits ring Farewell Canyon. After 2 miles the trail steepens and over the next mile ascends several switchbacks to the junction of the Franklin Pass Trail (Route 12). Stay in Farewell Canyon and

Hiking above Mineral King in one of the many beautiful alpine valleys and meadows along Route 13

continue south up a series of switchbacks to Farewell Gap. At Farewell Gap the trail leaves Sequoia National Park.

Mile 5.7 to 14.7 (Farewell Gap to Coyote Pass)

On the south side of Farewell Gap the trail follows the Little Kern River, descending from 10,587 feet to about 8800 feet over the first 3 miles. Here there is a trail junction; take the left fork, the Farewell–Coyote Pass Trail, as it leaves the Little Kern River and traverses Shotgun Creek and Pistol Creek before ascending to Coyote Pass. The trail crests about 0.5 mile to the west of Coyote Pass, where it gradually descends 280 feet to the pass. Overall, the trail loses 1900 feet and gains 2400 feet over 9 miles. The trail reenters Sequoia National Park at the pass.

Mile 14.7 to 20.6 (Coyote Pass to Kern Canyon)

From Coyote Pass, the trail descends 3700 feet over 5.9 miles to the Kern River and Kern Canyon Ranger Station. The descent is continuous but steepens markedly as the trail nears the Kern River. Kern Canyon is the low point on this route. Here the trail drops to a point nearly 1500 feet below the start of the trail at Mineral King. At Kern Canyon, one option is to turn north, following the Kern River Trail for 6 miles, thereby joining Routes 11 and 12. However, Route 13 continues northeast to Big Whitney Meadow and Siberian Pass.

Mile 20.6 to 37.1 (Kern Canyon to Siberian Pass)

It is a long, continuous climb out of Kern Canyon past the Natural Bridge, Little Whitney Meadow, and Big Whitney Meadow to Siberian Pass. The trail gains 4600 feet over 16.5 miles. On a more positive note, there are no sections that would be considered difficult or steep— just a persistent uphill grind to the pass.

Mile 37.1 to 43.6
(Siberian Pass to Lower Rock Creek Crossing)

Cross Siberian Pass to its north side and proceed across the upper portion of the Siberian Outpost, turning left on the Pacific Crest Trail. Descend to Rock Creek and the Rock Creek Patrol Cabin. There is a bear-proof food storage box at the trail crossing of Rock Creek.

Mile 43.6 to 46.4
(Lower Rock Creek Crossing to Guyot Pass)
Refer to Route 9 for a description of this segment of trail.

Mile 46.4 to 50 (Guyot Pass to Lower Crabtree Meadow)
Refer to Route 9 for a description of this segment of trail. There is a bear-proof food storage box in Lower Crabtree Meadow near the Pacific Crest Trail.

Mile 50 to 53.8 (Lower Crabtree Meadow to Guitar Lake)
Refer to Route 9 for a description of this segment of trail. A bear-proof food storage box is located in Crabtree Meadow south of the Crabtree Patrol Cabin near the stream crossing.

Mile 53.8 to 57.3 (Guitar Lake to Mount Whitney Trail)
Refer to Route 9 for a description of this segment of trail.

Mile 57.3 to 59.3
(Mount Whitney Trail to Mount Whitney summit)
Refer to Route 9 for a description of this segment of trail. After summiting, return to your pack at the junction of the John Muir Trail and the Mount Whitney Trail and descend the Mount Whitney Trail. For a description of the trail, refer to Route 6.

Appendix 1:
CALIFORNIA'S FOURTEENERS

This list was compiled from data contained in the newly photo-revised USGS 7.5-minute maps, Steve Roper's *The Climber's Guide to the High Sierra,* and R. J. Secor's *The High Sierra: Peaks, Passes and Trails.* The new 7.5-minute maps adjust many elevations from the older 15-minute maps, based on more accurate mapping techniques.

Determining which peaks to include in a list of the California fourteeners seems simple enough. However, it is not always readily apparent whether a given high point is a peak or merely a point or subpeak on the ridge leading to the main summit. To minimize the amount of subjectivity, I used several general selection guidelines: the peak should be named on the USGS maps or have a commonly used name, it should have an elevation rise of at least 400 feet above the land bridge (col or pass) connecting it with its closest neighbor peak, and it should be at least 0.5 mile from its neighbor peak. These guidelines were not applied blindly, but provided general parameters for selecting the 14,000-foot peaks.

The list in this appendix is arranged in descending order using the elevations of the new 7.5-minute USGS maps. Peaks measured in meters have been converted to feet by multiplying by 3.2808 (39.3701 inches per meter divided by 12 inches = 3.2808). Example: 4416.9 meters (the height of Whitney) = 14,490.97 feet.

The California fourteeners listed here include the thirteen peaks in California exceeding 14,000 feet and ten high points or subpeaks. These ten subpeaks are noted in the list by an alphanumeric designation such as 1a or 2b.

Rank	Peak Name	Elevation	Subpeak Elevation	Region and Mountain Range
1	Mount Whitney	14,491		Mount Whitney, Sierra Nevada
	1a. Keelers Needle		14,240+	
	1b. Crooks Peak			
	(Day Needle)		14,173+	
	1c. Third Needle		14,107+	
	1d. Aiguille Extra		14,042+	
2	Mount Williamson	14,370+		Mount Whitney, Sierra Nevada
	2a. West Horn		14,107+	
	2b. East Horn		14,042+	
3	White Mountain	14,246		White Mountain, White Mountains
4	North Palisade	14,242		Palisades, Sierra Nevada
	4a. Starlight Peak		14,180+	
	4b. Polemonium		14,080+	
5	Mount Shasta	14,162		Mount Shasta, Cascade
	5a. West Summit		14,040+	
6	Mount Sill	14,153		Palisades, Sierra Nevada
7	Mount Russell	14,088		Mount Whitney, Sierra Nevada
	7a. East Summit		14,042+	
8	Split Mountain	14,042		Palisades, Sierra Nevada
9	Mount Langley	14,022		Mount Whitney, Sierra Nevada
10	Mount Tyndall	14,019		Mount Whitney, Sierra Nevada
11	Middle Palisade	14,012		Palisades, Sierra Nevada
12	Mount Muir	14,012		Mount Whitney, Sierra Nevada
13	Thunderbolt Peak	14,003		Palisades, Sierra Nevada

Appendix 2
EQUIPMENT CHECKLISTS

EQUIPMENT CHECKLIST: MULTIDAY TRIPS

Individual Items

Map and compass

Internal frame pack

Sleeping bag to 20–25 degrees Fahrenheit

Sleeping pad

Lightweight gloves

Midweight polypropylene top

Powerstretch or microfleece vest

Fleece jacket with hood

Light, waterproof parka with hood

Lightweight polypropylene bottoms

Baggy nylon shorts

Wind pants with full-length zipper

Extra pair of wool-blend socks

Hat with sun visor

Cold-weather hat

Sunglasses

Plastic measuring cup (2-cup size) and spoon

Wide-mouth water bottles (2 litres)

Water purification tablets (iodine)

Headlamp or flashlight

Extra batteries

Inexpensive watch

Small trash bag

Personal toiletries: sunblock (SPF-50), lip balm, aloe vera gel, insect repellent, toilet paper, cleansing wipes, antibacterial waterless soap, toothbrush, toothpaste, bandanna, retractable scissors, pocket knife

Group Equipment

Hanging stove with cooking pot

2 lighters

Fuel canisters

Free-standing (2- or 3-pole) tent

First-aid kit: ibuprofen, moleskin, antibiotic, codeine, decongestant,
antacids, elastic bandage, 4-inch gauze pads, adhesive bandages,
butterfly bandages, adhesive tape, antibiotic ointment, first-aid
field manual (see Appendix 3 for a complete list)

Optional Items

Ski pole or walking stick

Ice ax

Crampons

Camera and film

Altimeter

Global positioning system (GPS)

Cellular phone

Notebook and pen

Reading material

Day pack

Light down jacket or down vest

Water filter

Mosquito repellent

Food Items

See Appendix 4: Menu Planner.

EQUIPMENT CHECKLIST: SINGLE-DAY HIKE

Individual Items

Map and compass

Day pack

Light gloves

Midweight polypropylene top

Powerstretch or microfleece vest

Fleece jacket with hood
Light, waterproof parka with hood
Lightweight polypropylene bottoms
Baggy nylon shorts
Wind pants with full-length zipper
Extra pair of wool-blend socks
Hat with sun visor
Sunglasses
Wide-mouth water bottles (2 litres)
Water purification tablets (iodine)
Headlamp or flashlight
Extra batteries
Inexpensive watch
Personal toiletries: sunblock (SPF-50), lip balm, aloe vera gel, insect repellent, toilet paper, cleansing wipes, antibacterial waterless soap, bandanna, retractable scissors, pocket knife

Group Equipment

First-aid kit: ibuprofen, moleskin, codeine, decongestant, antacids, elastic bandage, 4-inch gauze pads, adhesive bandages, butterfly bandages, adhesive tape, antibiotic ointment, first-aid field manual (see Appendix 3 for a complete list)

Optional Items

Ski pole or walking stick
Ice ax
Crampons
Camera and film
Altimeter
Global positioning system (GPS)
Cellular phone
Water filter
Mosquito repellent

Food Items

See Appendix 4 for lunch suggestions.

THE TEN ESSENTIALS

Extra clothing
Extra food
Sunglasses
Knife
Firestarter
First-aid kit
Matches in a waterproof container, or lighter
Flashlight
Map
Compass

Appendix 3
CONTENTS OF A WILDERNESS FIRST-AID KIT
(by Colin Fuller, M.D.)

Mountaineering first aid begins with the understanding that it is the responsibility of every hiker and climber to have complete knowledge of basic first-aid practices and the ability to properly care for an injured partner in the wilderness. All hikers and climbers should take basic first-aid training offered by the Red Cross and mountaineering first-aid offered by many mountain guides. All parties should carry a first-aid kit with them. The kit should be small, compact, sturdy, and waterproof. A small plastic box with a tight lid makes a good container. All medications should be marked clearly, including dosage and expiration dates.

The following first-aid kit list has been developed for use on backcountry wilderness trips of 3 to 10 days. The number of items included in your first-aid kit can be pared back for shorter trips.

First-Aid Item	Application
Ibuprofen, 200 mg	For aches, minor pain, joint and muscle stiffness, headache, fever
Personal medications	For asthma, diabetes, allergies, and other conditions
Codeine	For severe pain
Antibiotics	For bronchitis and urinary tract infections
Sulfacetamide 10 percent solution	For an inflamed, purulent eye
Diamox 125 mg	For altitude sickness
Antacid tablets	For nausea and upset stomach
Antidiarrheal agents	For diarrhea or loose bowels
Metronidazole	For severe, prolonged diarrhea when giardiasis is suspected

First-Aid Item	Application
Decongestants	For congestion and hayfever
Moleskin	To prevent and protect blisters
2- x 4.5-inch adhesive bandages	To cover and protect cuts and lacerations
Butterfly bandages	To close lacerations
2-inch roll of stretch gauze	For hard-to-bandage areas
2-inch roll of adhesive cloth tape	To wrap sprains and secure dressings
Aloe vera gel	For sunburn and windburn, dry skin
Mild antiseptic soap or hydrogen peroxide	To clean abrasions and wounds
Topical antibiotic ointment	For minor abrasions and wounds
1 percent hydrocortisone ointment	For rashes, burns, and severe sunburn
Scissors	To cut bandages, moleskin, and tape
First-aid field manual	For reference and guidance

Appendix 4
MENU PLANNER

This Menu Planner includes easy-to-fix, tasty, and inexpensive alpine cuisine for breakfast, lunch, and dinner. All food items can be purchased at your local grocery store and are superior to costly freeze-dried backpacking meals. As a general rule, plan 2 pounds of food per person per day. The Menu Planner includes weights of each item and totals per person per day. Adjust the portions based on the appetites of those in your party. Throw in a couple of extra soups for emergency rations. To spice up your menu, bring a small spice kit. It is practically weightless and invaluable in creating palatable entrees. Include a small amount of seasoned salt, seasoned pepper, a few bouillon cubes, and a few cloves of fresh garlic. Cinnamon is nice as well. Bon appétit!

BREAKFAST (PER PERSON)

Weight	Food Item
2 ounces	Instant oatmeal, cream of wheat, or soup mix (in single-serving envelopes)
1 ounce	Add 2 tablespoons protein powder, powdered milk, and any combination of raisins, dried fruit, sunflower seeds, and mixed nuts to hot cereal
2 ounces	Nutritional bar that balances protein, carbohydrates, and fat
1 ounce	Hot drinks such as flavored coffee, spiced cider, or eggnog (in single-serving envelopes)
6 ounces	*Breakfast subtotal*

LUNCH (PER PERSON)

6 ounces	Bagel with cheese or crackers and peanut butter
2 ounces	Mixed nuts (cashews, almonds, pecans, brazil nuts, carob-covered raisins)
1.5 ounces	Chocolate candies or candy bar

1 ounce	Dried fruit
2.5 ounces	Sport drink (powder mix)
13 ounces	*Lunch subtotal*

DINNER (SERVES TWO)

2.5 ounces	Packaged soups
1 ounce	Add a fresh carrot and bell pepper or dried carrot bits
5 ounces	Instant packaged dinners such as pasta or beans and rice
1 ounce	Add protein powder, olive oil, and dried peas to the main course
6 ounces	Add 3- or 5-ounce can of chicken, tuna, turkey, or salmon
2.5 ounces	Sport drink (powder mix)
2 ounces	Hot drink: herbal tea, flavored coffee, spiced cider, or eggnog
3 ounces	Irish cream or amaretto
3 ounces	Two candy bars or cookies for dessert
26 ounces/2	*Dinner for two subtotal (13 ounces per person)*

SNACKS (SELECT ONE)

2 ounces	Potato chips, packaged in a cardboard cylinder for protection, or
2 ounces	Beef or turkey jerky, or
2 ounces	String cheese and crackers
2 ounces	*Snack subtotal*
34 ounces	**Grand total (per person, per day)**

Appendix 5
USEFUL CONTACTS AND RESOURCES

GENERAL INFORMATION

Backcountry Resource Center
Information for hikers, climbers, and backcountry skiers and snow-
boarders wishing to explore the mountains of California, the United
States, Canada, and beyond.
> Website: *http://pweb.jps.net/~prichins/backcountry_resource_*
> *center.htm*
> Email: *prichins@jps.net*

U.S. FOREST SERVICE: INYO NATIONAL FOREST

Campground Reservations
Many Forest Service campgrounds are first-come, first-served, but some
can be reserved.
> Website: *www.reserveusa.com*
> Phone: 800-280-2267
> TDD: 877-833-6777
> International calls: 518-885-3639

Permit Reservations
Permits for Mount Whitney Trail (Route 6) are issued through a lottery, and permit applications must be postmarked in February. For
all other Inyo National Forest trails (Routes 1–5 and 7–9), reservations can be made up to six months in advance of your departure
date. Mail or fax your reservation to:

Inyo National Forest Wilderness Reservation Office
873 North Main Street
Bishop, CA 93514
Fax: 760-873-2484

Wilderness Permits, Trail Conditions, Maps, Books, and Other Information

Inyo National Forest
Mount Whitney Ranger Station
P.O. Box 8
640 South Main Street
Lone Pine, CA 93545
Phone: 760-876-6200
Wilderness Information Line: 760-873-2408
Website: *www.r5.fs.fed.us/inyo*

NATIONAL PARKS: SEQUOIA AND KINGS CANYON NATIONAL PARKS

Campground Reservations

Most Sequoia and Kings Canyon National Park campgrounds are first-come, first-served, but some can be reserved.
Website: *reservations.nps.gov*
Phone: 800-365-2267
TDD: 888-530-9796
International calls: 301-722-1257

Sequoia and Kings Canyon National Parks (Routes 10–13)

Wilderness permits (reservations can be made beginning on March 1 of each year).
47050 Generals Highway
HCR 89 Box 60
Three Rivers, CA 93271-9700
Wilderness Office phone: 559-565-3341 or 559-565-3766
Fax: 559-565-4239
Website: *www.nps.gov/seki*
General information phone line: 559-565-3341 (for 24-hour recorded information on roads, weather, campgrounds, and lodging or to reach a park ranger)

Sequoia Natural History Association

Natural history, maps, books, Pear Lake Hut reservations (winter use only), and other information.

HCR 89 Box 10
Three Rivers, CA 93271
Phone: 559-565-3759
Website: *www.sequoiahistory.org*

Lodgepole: Sequoia National Park

Pick up wilderness permits for the High Sierra Trail (Route 11) at the Lodgepole Ranger Station (phone 559-565-3775).

For the Lodgepole Visitor Center, call 559-565-3782. The nearby area includes the Giant Forest Museum, Nature Center, Crystal Cave, food, shops, market, deli, gift shop, snack bar, horseback riding, showers, laundry, lodging, and bear-proof canisters. Nearby are picnic areas and campgrounds: Lodgepole (204 sites) and Dorst (201 sites). For lodging, call 888-252-5757.

Mineral King: Sequoia National Park

Pick up wilderness permits for the Franklin Pass Trail (Route 12) and Farewell Gap Trail (Route 13) at the Mineral King Ranger Station (phone 559-565-3768).

Atwell Mill has 21 campground sites, and Cold Springs has 40 campground sites.

The Silver City Resort (privately owned), located about 7 miles from the trailhead, includes a store, restaurant, and lodging (phone 559-561-3223).

Roads End and Cedar Grove: Kings Canyon National Park

Pick up wilderness permits for Bubbs Creek Trail (Route 10) at the Roads End Ranger Station (no phone).

For the Cedar Grove Visitor Center (6 miles west of Roads End) and Ranger Station, call 559-565-3793.

The area includes a store, market, restaurant, gift shop, and bear-proof canisters.

There are four campgrounds in the Roads End and Cedar Grove area: Sentinel (83 sites), Sheep Creek (111 sites), Canyon View (23 sites), and Moraine (120 sites).

For lodging, call 559-335-5500.

SOURCES FOR MAPS

Maps can be purchased at the Inyo National Forest and the Sequoia and Kings Canyon National Park offices and at backpacking and outdoor stores. Additional sources are noted here.

Tom Harrison Maps
2 Falmouth Cove
San Rafael, CA 94901
Phone: 415-456-7940 or 800-265-9090
Website: *www.tomharrisonmaps.com*

U.S. Geological Survey Maps
USGS Information Services
Box 25286, Federal Center
Denver, CO 80225
Phone: 800-HELP-MAP
Website: *www.nmd.usgs.gov*

Wilderness Press
2440 Bancroft Way
Berkeley, CA, 94704
Phone: 510-843-8080 or 800-443-7227
Website: *www.wildernesspress.com*

Wildflower Productions, TOPO! Interactive Maps on CD-ROM
375 Alabama Street, Suite 230
San Francisco, CA 94110
Phone: 415-558-8700
Email: *info@topo.com*
Website: *www.topo.com*

TRAILHEAD SHUTTLE SERVICES

Kountry Korners
771 North Main Street #59
Bishop, CA 93514
Phone: 877-656-0756 (toll free) or 760-872-3951 (local)
Email: *trailshuttle@yahoo.com*

They will meet you at your exit point and drive you to the trailhead to start your hike. They rent and sell bear-proof canisters.

Wilder House Bed and Breakfast and Shuttle Service
HCR 67, Box 275 (325 Dust Lane)
Fort Independence, CA 93526
Phone: 760-878-2119 or 888-313-0151 (toll free)
Email: *wilder@wilderhouse.com*
Website: *www.wilderhouse.com*

Walt's Inyo Trailhead Transportation
P.O. Box 539
Lone Pine, CA 93545
Phone: 760-876-0035 or 760-876-5518

Inyo–Mono Transit
Phone: 760-872-1901

CALIFORNIA ROAD CONDITIONS

Caltrans (24-hour recorded message)
Phone: 916-445-7623 (ROAD) or 800-427-7623 (ROAD)

Mount Whitney as viewed from the Whitney Portal Road near Whitney Portal

Appendix 6
A BRIEF HISTORY: FACTS, FIGURES, AND FIRSTS

July 2, 1864: The Whitney Survey Field Party (Professor William Brewer, Yale; James Gardiner, Yale; Clarence King, Yale; Richard Cotter; and Charles Hoffman) first sighted Mount Whitney from the summit of Mount Brewer.

August 18, 1873: Albert Johnson, John Lucas, and Charles Begole (three Lone Pine fishermen) made the first ascent.

August 20, 1873: William Crapo and Abe Leyda made their ascent. Crapo claimed a first ascent on August 15, 1873, but the evidence is not convincing. The likely date of the climb is August 20, 1873.

September 6, 1873: William Hunter, Carl Rabe, William Crapo, and Tom McDonough completed the third ascent.

September 19, 1873: Clarence King and Frank Knowles were the fourth party to climb the peak.

October 21, 1873: John Muir made the first ascent of the Mountaineers Route.

1875: John Muir made the first ascent of the north face above Arctic Lakes.

1878: Mary Martin, Anna Mills, Hope Broughton, and Mrs. R. C. Redd were the first women to climb Whitney.

1881: Professor Samuel Langley, director of the Allegheny Observatory, made the first scientific expedition.

1904: G. P. Marsh of Lone Pine supervised construction of the Mount Whitney Trail. Funds were raised by the people of Lone Pine.

1909: G. P. Marsh supervised and completed the construction of the summit hut for the Smithsonian Institution.

1929: Dr. F. Zwickey made the first ski ascent.

August 16, 1931: Norman Clyde, Robert L. M. Underhill, Glen Dawson, and Jules Eichorn made the first technical climb on the east face.

September 5, 1937: Robert Brinton, Glen Dawson, Muir Dawson, Richard Jones, and Howard Koster first climbed the East Buttress.

1974: Galen Rowell was the first to complete a ski descent of the Mountaineers Route, 101 years after John Muir first climbed the route.

1983: Allan Bard and Tom Carter made the first ski descent of the north face, 108 years after John Muir first climbed the route.

TRAIL USE DATA

The Mount Whitney Trail is by far the most popular trail to Whitney's summit as 150 day hikers and 50 overnight backpackers are issued permits daily. The following are some statistics about the number of hikers receiving permits for the Mount Whitney Trail for various selected years. The information was provided by Jan Cutts of the U.S. Forest Service.

Year	Day Use	Overnight Use	Total
1986	n/a	7,411	n/a
1988	n/a	10,175	n/a
1989	6,491	12,630	19,121
1993	n/a	3,693	n/a
1996	7,532	8,382	15,914
1997	11,350	8,446	20,416
1998	13,236	9,066	22,302
1999	14,086	9,753	23,839
2000	13,570*	10,840*	24,410

*These numbers include partial season actual use for 2000 plus an estimate for the remainder of the hiking season.

Year 2000 Lottery

In the first season of the lottery conducted for the Mount Whitney Trail in February 2000, the U.S. Forest Service received 3960 wilderness permit applications representing about 15,000 people. Of this total, 2674 permit applications (approximately 10,000 people) were granted and 1286 applications (about 5000 people) were rejected.

Totals for All Trails

Mount Whitney has become an exceedingly popular destination. It is by far the most popular peak in California. Here is a rundown of the number of hikers receiving a permit to ascend the peak from various hiking trails and climbing routes. Each year, approximately 30,000 hikers receive a wilderness permit to hike the peak each year, but less than one-third reach the summit.

Trail	1998	2000
Mount Whitney Trail, day use	13,236	13,570*
Mount Whitney Trail, overnight	9,066	10,840*
North Fork Lone Pine Creek, day use (estimate)	2,720	3,400*
North Fork Lone Pine Creek, overnight	1,863	2,330*
Various other Inyo National Forest trails (estimate)	2,000	—
Kearsarge Pass Trail	—	530*
Shepherd Pass Trail	—	80*
New Army Pass Route	—	890*
Cottonwood Pass Trail	—	450*
Others (estimate)	—	100
John Muir Trail starting at Yosemite (estimate)	200	200
Pacific Crest Trail (estimate of those reaching the summit)	200	200
Various trails originating west of the crest (estimate)	200	200
Totals	29,485	32,790

*These numbers include partial season actual use for 2000 plus an estimate for the remainder of the hiking season.

NUMBER OF HIKERS AND CLIMBERS REACHING THE SUMMIT

The popularity of the peak has been growing, as evidenced by those recording their names in the summit register over the past 40 years. Much of the following data were provided by Ward Eldridge, Sequoia National Park, based on archived summit registers.

Year	Names in Register
1957	2658
1959	5490
1969	8869
1979	6560
1988	6200
1989	5800
1997	9760
1998	8100*
1999	9520
2000	10,240

*The low 1998 number may be attributed to the exceptionally heavy winter snow that blocked the trails well into the summer.

Appendix 7
GLOSSARY

arête A sharp, narrow ridge.

cairn (rock cairn or rock duck) Three or more rocks placed on top of each other to mark a trail or cross-country route; a conical heap of stones built as a monument or landmark.

cirque A steep, hollow excavation high on a mountainside made by glacial erosion; a natural amphitheater.

climber's trail or use trail A route that has evolved over the years through the use of many hikers and climbers heading toward a common objective such as a remote mountain pass, peak, or alpine lake.

col A gap or notch between high points or between two peaks along a ridge. A col is similar to a high mountain pass.

couloir A deep mountain gash, gully, or chute, usually but not always leading to a col.

cross-country travel Travel in the backcountry without benefit of a maintained trail.

edema An abnormal collection of fluid in some part of the body, as in pulmonary edema (an abnormal collection of fluid in the air sacs of the lungs) or cerebral edema (an abnormal collection of fluid in the skull cavity).

fourteener A peak higher than 14,000 feet in elevation.

John Muir Trail (JMT) The John Muir Trail begins in Yosemite Valley and ends on the summit of Mount Whitney. The Pacific Crest Trail and John Muir Trail are the same trail for much of the length of the John Muir Trail. In this guidebook, where the two trails share a common route, the trail is called the John Muir Trail.

High Sierra Trail (HST) The High Sierra Trail starts at Crescent Meadow in Sequoia National Park, crosses the Great Western Divide at Kaweah Gap, and descends to the Kern River before joining the John Muir Trail at Wallace Creek—a distance of about 50 miles.

moraine A mass of rocks, gravel, sand, and clay carried and deposited by a glacier, along its side (lateral moraine), at its lower end (terminal moraine), or beneath the ice and snow (ground moraine).

Mount Whitney Zone A 15-square-mile area designation surrounding Mount Whitney, jointly managed by the Inyo National Forest and Sequoia and Kings Canyon National Parks. Because of heavy usage, this zone has special quotas for day hikers and backpackers. The quotas in this zone are in effect from May 15 through November 1. Mount Whitney hikers must secure permission to enter the Mount Whitney Zone when they request their wilderness permits.

National Park Service (NPS) The National Park Service administers and manages four national parks in California (Lassen Volcanic, Yosemite, Sequoia, and Kings Canyon National Parks).

Pacific Crest Trail (PCT) The Pacific Crest Trail system stretches from the Canadian border to Mexico. The PCT and John Muir Trail are the same trail for much of the length of the John Muir Trail. In this guidebook, where they share a common route, the trail is called the John Muir Trail.

powerstretch fleece A close-fitting, stretchy insulation.

scree Small rocks and sand deposited below cliffs or steep mountain slopes, caused by erosion and decay of mountain slopes.

talus Large rock, boulders, and debris deposited at the base of a cliff; a mantle of rock fragments on a slope below a steep rock face.

tarn A small mountain lake or pond, especially one that fills a cirque.

traverse To move across a mountain slope in an oblique manner (slanting or contouring, diagonal to the slope).

United States Forest Service (USFS) The U.S. Forest Service manages the national forests and wilderness areas in California.

United States Geological Survey (USGS) Maps Maps published and distributed by the USGS that show elevation and contour lines. The USGS is responsible for the National Mapping Program.

wilderness permits Permits are required year-round on all trails included in this guidebook. During heavy usage periods, these trails are also subject to permit limits or quotas. Wilderness permit reservations are recommended for trips beginning during the quota season; see Chapter 4 for details.

Appendix 8
SELECTED BIBLIOGRAPHY AND REFERENCES

Crapsey, Malinee, ed. *Backcountry Basics* and *The Sequoia Bark: Summer 1999 Park and Forest Guide*. Newspaper-type publications of the Sequoia Natural History Association and Sequoia and Kings Canyon National Parks, Three Rivers, CA.

Graydon, Don and Kurt Hanson, eds. *Mountaineering: The Freedom of the Hills*, 6th ed. The Mountaineers, Seattle, WA, 1997.

Hellweg, Paul and Scott McDonald. *Mount Whitney Guide for Hikers and Climbers*, Canyon Publishing Company, Canoga Park, CA, 1994.

King, Clarence. *Mountaineering in the Sierra Nevada*, published by James R. Osgood & Company, 1872 and 1874. Reprinted by the University of Nebraska Press, Lincoln, 1971.

Miller, Dorcas S. *Backcountry Cooking: From Pack to Plate in 10 Minutes*, The Mountaineers, Seattle, WA, 1998.

Moynier, John and Claude Fiddler. *Sierra Classics: 100 Best Climbs in the High Sierra*, Falcon Press, Helena, MT, 1993.

Muir, John. "The Cañon of the South Fork of Kings River: A Rival of the Yosemite," *Century Illustrated Monthly Magazine*, vol. 43, pp. 77–97, November 1891.

Muir, John. "Exhibit." Website maintained by Harold Wood and Harvey Chinn. *www.sierraclub.org/john_muir_exhibit*.

Muir, John. *Our National Parks*. In *John Muir: The Eight Wilderness-Discovery Books*, The Mountaineers, Seattle, WA, 1995.

Muir, John. "Snow-Storm on Mount Shasta," *Harper's New Monthly Magazine*, September 1877.

Prater, Yvonne and Ruth Dyar Mendenhall. *Gorp, Glop and Glue Stew: Favorite Foods from 165 Outdoor Experts*, The Mountaineers, Seattle, WA, 1981.

Rébuffat, Gaston. *On Snow and Rock*. New York: Oxford University Press, 1968.

Richins, Paul Jr. *50 Classic Backcountry Ski and Snowboard Summits in California: Mount Shasta to Mount Whitney,* The Mountaineers, Seattle, WA, 1999.

Roper, Steve. *The Climber's Guide to the High Sierra,* Sierra Club Books, San Francisco, CA.

Secor, R. J. *The High Sierra: Peaks, Passes and Trails,* The Mountaineers, Seattle, WA, second edition, 1999.

Sequoia and Kings Canyon National Parks staff. "Wilderness Food Storage Box Locations," National Park Service, 1999.

Sequoia and Kings Canyon National Parks staff. "Official Map and Guide: Sequoia and Kings Canyon National Parks," National Park Service, 1999.

Steele, Peter, M.D. *Backcountry Medical Guide,* The Mountaineers, Seattle, WA, 1999.

Wheelock, Walt and Tom Condon. *Climbing Mount Whitney,* La Siesta Press, Glendale, CA, revised edition, 1970.

Wilkerson, James A. *Medicine for Mountaineering,* The Mountaineers, Seattle, WA, second edition, 1975.

INDEX

ABOUT THE AUTHOR

Paul Richins was raised in Weaverville, California, and started hiking in the Trinity Alps at age 12. He has more than thirty-five years of wilderness experience backpacking, mountain climbing, ski mountaineering, and white-water kayaking.

As a longtime member of the American Alpine Club and the Sierra Club, he has participated in a number of major expeditions to Alaska (West Ridge of Mount Hunter and the South Ridge of Saint Elias), Canada (East Ridge of Mount Logan), Argentina (Cerro Aconcagua), and Tibet (Cho Oyu, the sixth-highest peak in the world). Richins and two climbing partners completed the first ascent of the Southwest Ridge of Stortind, an impressive peak in the Lyngen Alps of northern Norway. He plans to climb Mount Everest in 2002.

In addition, he has climbed many other peaks in Norway, Argentina, Canada, Ecuador, and the western United States. He has hiked extensively throughout the Sierra Nevada and has climbed hundreds of peaks in California. He has climbed Mount Whitney by the various routes detailed in this guidebook and has completed a ski ascent and descent of Mount Whitney's Mountaineers Route.

The author on the summit of Mount Saint Helens with Mount Rainier in the background. Photo by Sierra Richins

Richins is author of the highly successful ski mountaineering guidebook *50 Classic Backcountry Ski and Snowboard Summits in California: Mount Shasta to Mount Whitney.* He also maintains the Backcountry Resource Center, a website of valuable information for the backcountry skier, climber, or hiker wishing to explore the mountains of California, the United States, Canada, and beyond.

Professionally, Richins is an economist working as a project manager at the California Energy Commission, overseeing the work of a multidisciplinary team of engineers, planners, and environmental scientists. He lives in El Dorado Hills, California, with his daughter, Sierra Nicole Richins.

Richins is interested in your feedback and encourages your comments on the book. His email address is *prichins@jps.net,* and his website is *http://pweb.jps.net/~prichins/backcountry_resource_center.htm.*

THE MOUNTAINEERS, founded in 1906, is a nonprofit outdoor activity and conservation club whose mission is "to explore, study, preserve, and enjoy the natural beauty of the outdoors. . . ." Based in Seattle, Washington, the club is now the third-largest such organization in the United States, with 15,000 members and five branches throughout Washington State.

The Mountaineers sponsors both classes and year-round outdoor activities in the Pacific Northwest, which include hiking, mountain climbing, ski-touring, snowshoeing, bicycling, camping, kayaking and canoeing, nature study, sailing, and adventure travel. The club's conservation division supports environmental causes through educational activities, sponsoring legislation, and presenting informational programs. All club activities are led by skilled, experienced volunteers, who are dedicated to promoting safe and responsible enjoyment and preservation of the outdoors.

If you would like to participate in these organized outdoor activities or the club's programs, consider a membership in The Mountaineers. For information and an application, write or call The Mountaineers, Club Headquarters, 300 Third Avenue West, Seattle, WA 98119; 206-284-6310.

The Mountaineers Books, an active, nonprofit publishing program of the club, produces guidebooks, instructional texts, historical works, natural history guides, and works on environmental conservation. All books produced by The Mountaineers Books fulfill the club's mission.

Send or call for our catalog of more than 450 outdoor titles:

The Mountaineers Books
1001 SW Klickitat Way, Suite 201
Seattle, WA 98134
800-553-4453
mbooks@mountaineers.org
www.mountaineersbooks.org

The Mountaineers Books is proud to be a corporate sponsor of Leave No Trace, whose mission is to promote and inspire responsible outdoor recreation through education, research, and partnerships. The Leave No Trace program is focused specifically on human-powered (non-motorized) recreation.

Leave No Trace strives to educate visitors about the nature of their recreational impacts, as well as offer techniques to prevent and minimize such impacts. Leave No Trace is best understood as an educational and ethical program, not as a set of rules and regulations.

For more information, visit *www.LNT.org*, or call 800-332-4100.

Other titles you may enjoy from The Mountaineers Books:

MOUNTAINEERING: Freedom of the Hills, Sixth Edition,
The Mountaineers
The completely revised and expanded edition of the best-selling mountaineering book of all time—required reading for all climbers.

75 YEAR-ROUND HIKES IN NORTHERN CALIFORNIA, *Marc Soares*
Avoid the crowds and observe nature scenery you've never before encountered. Marc Soares introduces seventy-five hikes from Mount Shasta to Big Sur that are easily accessible and at their peak in fall, winter and spring.

75 HIKES IN™ CALIFORNIA'S LASSEN PARK & MOUNT SHASTA REGION, *John R. Soares*
Offers a variety of hikes in some of the most popular hiking spots in the Golden State ranging from day-hikes to extended backpack trips.

100 CLASSIC HIKES IN™ NORTHERN CALIFORNIA, Second Edition,
John R. Soares & Marc J. Soares
A full-color hiking guide written by experts who have personally researched every trail. Includes a mix of day hikes and overnight backpacking trips.

100 HIKES IN™ CALIFORNIA'S CENTRAL SIERRA & COAST RANGE,
Vicky Spring
A comprehensive guide to the most scenic trails of Yosemite and Sequoia Kings Canyon National Parks, Pinnacles National Monument, and the John Muir, Ansel Adams, Emigrant, and Hoover Wildernesses.

SELECTED CLIMBS IN THE CASCADES, Vol II: Alpine Routes, Sport Climbs & Crag Climbs, *Jim Nelson and Peter Potterfield*
Volume two of this classic guide adds one hundred additional routes. A great mix of walk-ups, scrambles, and rock, ice, crag, and sport climbs for all skill levels.

BACKPACKER'S **EVERYDAY WISDOM: 1001 Expert Tips for Hikers,**
Karen Berger
Expert tips and tricks for hikers and backpackers selected from one of the most popular *Backpacker* magazine columns.